WHAT GRACE THEY RECEIVED

Worship Commemorations
For 12 Ancient And
Modern Saints

BY THOMAS A. RENQUIST

C.S.S. Publishing Co., Inc.
Lima, Ohio

Copyright © 1993 by
The C.S.S. Publishing Company, Inc.
Lima, Ohio

All rights reserved. If you are the original purchaser, you may copy the material which precedes each reading (worship material for worship use; educational material for classroom use). The material you may copy includes a listing of the text, hymn of the day, prayer of the day and other related material. No other part of this publication may be reproduced, stored in a retrieval system, or transmitted in any form or by any means, electronic, mechanical, photocopying, recording, or otherwise, without the prior permission of the publisher. Inquiries should be addressed to: The C.S.S. Publishing Company, Inc., 628 South Main Street, Lima, Ohio 45804.

Library of Congress Cataloging-in-Publication Data

Renquist, Thomas A., 1947-
    What grace they received : worship commemorations for 12 ancient and modern saints / Thomas A. Renquist.
        108 p.   14 by 21.5 cm.
    Includes bibliographical references.
    ISBN 1-55673-567-7
    1. Christian biography — Prayer-books and devotions — English. 2. Worship programs. I. Title
BR1600.2.R39   1992
265'.9—dc20   92-40150
                                                                                                      CIP

9314 / ISBN 1-55673-567-7   PRINTED IN U.S.A.

To my wife, Christine

Table Of Contents

Introduction

It is also taught among us that saints should be kept in remembrance so that our faith may be strengthened when we see what grace they received and how they were sustained by faith. Moreover, their good works are to be an example for us, each of us in his own calling.

— Article XXI, Augsburg Confession

Yes, Virgina, there really are such persons as saints! The Augsburg confessors back in 1530 may have warned against praying to the saints, but they were not about to do away with them. Instead, the saints are lifted up as role models for us — examples of good works, certainly; but even more than that, examples of how God works through people: "See what grace they received."

With the introduction of the *Lutheran Book of Worship* in 1978, American Lutherans were reminded that the ranks of saints are ever-increasing. A calendar of commemorations was provided — saints from every century down to the present, men and women who can be examples for us of good works empowered by God's grace.

I have chosen 12 of these "commemorated saints" and have developed worship resources for their day of commemoration. Eight of these days of commemoration will fall upon a Sunday in 1993: Cyril and Methodius, Perpetua and Felicity, Thomas Aquinas, Athanasius, Ludwig Nommensen, Benedict of Nursia, Ignatius and John Christian Frederick Heyer. The remaining four will fall upon a Sunday in 1994: Wilhelm Loehe, Bartolome' de Las Casas, Albert Schweitzer and Dag Hammarskjold.

Even though this *Lutheran Book of Worship* calendar of commemorations was put together by Lutherans, it has enjoyed a popularity among all Christians. In fact, only two of the 12 "commemorated saints" in this book — Heyer and Loehe — had any official connection to a Lutheran church.

In most instances, the main worship resource is designed for "the sermon slot" (the one exception is the entire litany developed for the commemoration of Dag Hammarskjold). And yet these are not sermons in the traditional sense. They are designed for two or more readers: one reader serves as the narrator; a second reader will often share excerpts from the writings of the saints; occasionally, there are additional readers (for example, a reader who will make connections to our lives today).

In addition, I have made suggestions for possible scripture texts, hymn of the day, prayer of the day (the brief collect used in liturgical churches), and a petition to be included in the prayers (the longer prayer of intercessions which follows the sermon in many churches). These resources are intended for use in the Sunday morning worship service, but certainly could be utilized in other contexts as well (for example, mid-week Lenten services).

I make no pretense of having conducted exhaustive primary research; rather, I have made much use of secondary resources, shaping them into a form that I hope will make these saints accessible to the worshiping community.

The great bulk of this project was completed during a three-month sabbatical during the summer of 1991 — a much appreciated gift from the congregation I serve, Good Shepherd Lutheran Church, Rochester, Minnesota, along with financial assistance from the Southeastern Minnesota Synod of the Evangelical Lutheran Church in America. My wife, Christine, deserves the most thanks for her invaluable editing suggestions and especially for her patient tutoring of this "techno-moron" in his first introduction to a Macintosh computer!

Of course, we are all saints; we have all been made saints of our God through the grace of our Lord Jesus Christ. But even we saints need heroes, examples, and role models, for our continuing pilgrimage in the faith. Whether it's Saint Ignatius from the first century or Saint Dag Hammarskjold from the 20th century, I hope your faith may be strengthened when you see "what grace they received."

Thomas A. Renquist
Feast of Mary, Mother of Our Lord
August 15, 1991

8

Wilhelm Loehe, The Great
Heart Of Neuendettelsau

Date: January 2

Text: 1 Timothy 4:12b-16

Hymn Of The Day: *(Written by Loehe; can be sung to the tune of Erhalt Uns, Herr, "LBW" No. 230):*

Lord Jesus Christ, with us abide,
For it is now toward eventide;
And let Thy Word, that light divine,
Continue in our midst to shine.

Our heart's true comfort is Thy Word,
And well it shields Thy Church, dear Lord;
So let us in Thy Word abide,
That we may seek no other guide.

Thus keep us in Thy Word, we pray,
While we continue on our way,
And help us, when this life is o'er,
To be with Thee forevermore.

Prayer Of The Day: *(The following was written by Loehe for use as the prayer of the day during the Christmas season.)*
Help us, Lord God, that we, being released from our old sinful birth, may be made partakers of the new birth in the flesh of Thy beloved Son, and ever continue in the same; through Thy Son, Jesus Christ, our Lord. Amen.

9

A Litany For The Lord's Prayer *(written by Loehe):*

OUR FATHER,
>   in-superable in creation,
>   sweet in love,
>   rich in every heritage!

WHO ART IN HEAVEN,
>   a mirror of eternity,
>   the crown of joy.
>   the treasure of eternal salvation!

HALLOWED BE THY NAME,
>   that it be like honey upon the tongue,
>   a harp unto our ears,
>   a devotion in our hearts!

THY KINGDOM COME,
>   joyfully, without perversion;
>   quietly, without sorrow;
>   safely, beyond possibility to lose it!

THY WILL BE DONE ON EARTH AS IT IS IN HEAVEN,
>   that we hate whatever displeases Thee;
>   love what Thou lovest;
>   and fulfill all things that are pleasing to Thee!

GIVE US THIS DAY OUR DAILY BREAD,
>   the bread of
>>   knowledge,
>>   penitence,
>>   pardon
>   and every need of our bodies.

FORGIVE US OUR TRESPASSES, AS WE FORGIVE THOSE WHO TRESPASS AGAINST US;
>   forgive us our trespasses against Thee, against our fellow-men and against ourselves, which we have multiplied either through the commission of wrongs

or the omission to do the good we ought to do, as we forgive all who have despised or offended us by word or deed, by giving or taking away from us, spiritually or temporally.

AND LEAD US NOT INTO TEMPTATION,
    of the world,
    the flesh,
    or the devil.

BUT DELIVER US FROM EVIL,
    both temporal and spiritual,
    and from all sorrows in time and eternity.

AMEN.

Prayers:

In thankfulness for your faithful shepherd of souls, Wilhelm Loehe, that we too may praise you in our worship, seek peace and unity in the church, and give ourselves wholeheartedly to the mission of the church in the world.

Wilhelm Loehe

The Great Heart Of Neuendettelsau

Reader 1: In 1808 in Germany, Wilhelm Loehe was born into a pious Christian family with deep roots in the Lutheran church. At the very early age of eight, Loehe decided that he would become a pastor; and his mother, by then a widow, saw to it that he received the necessary education.

The Lutheran Church in Germany at this time was still very much dominated by rationalism, a movement which emphasized the mind over the spirit and neglected the evangelical and missionary thrust of the church. At the time of his ordination, Loehe wrote:

Reader 2: "Since in our time there is no lack of candidates who are completely devoid of evangelical faith and life but still desire ordination and want to bear the name of Evangelical Lutheran ministers, I cannot help but declare that I definitely do not want to be included in this group. By God's help I shall preach the true doctrine and not be silent until the Lord himself takes me, his peace-loving soldier, out of the church militant into the blessed quietude of the church triumphant."

Reader 1: No parishes were immediately available to Loehe, so for the next seven years he served a variety of vicarages, working under more experienced pastors. He soon drew attention as an outstanding preacher, but at the same time he acquired the reputation of a "troublemaker" — one who would speak plainly about sin wherever he saw it, no matter whose toes were stepped on. The feathers of church authorities, too, were ruffled more than once. All this only delayed his first call to a parish.

Finally, however, it came: a call to serve the church at Neuendettelsau, a poor peasant community. Earlier Loehe had commented that he wouldn't want his dog buried in that town. Yet he accepted the call and spent the rest of his ministry in that tiny village.

Loehe's preaching was always gospel-centered, focusing on sin, grace and love; and it continued to draw large crowds from the surrounding countryside. He put considerable effort into his sermon-writing:

Reader 2: "With suffering must I bring forth my sermons. From Monday until Sunday I work during the first hours of the day on the sermon. I sigh, pray and fear until I mount the pulpit — and then God's grace is made new."

Reader 1: However, it wasn't just the sermon, but the entire liturgy which commanded Loehe's attention. Very patiently and slowly he introduced a number of changes into the liturgy at Neuendettelsau. For example, he spent 10 years introducing a full communion liturgy. His congregation returned to the ancient tradition of celebrating the Eucharist every Sunday. Worship, in Loehe's view, was the most important part of a congregation's life:

Reader 2: "In the worship services the congregation feels itself closest to its Lord. There, as close to the Bridegroom as it can get, it leads a heavenly life on earth, an earthly life in heaven."

Reader 1: Another major part of his ministry was pastoral care, visiting the sick and the dying. He also reintroduced the practice of private confession before receiving holy communion. Loehe believed that the job of the pastor was to practice "seelsorge," the care of souls.

However, Loehe's greatest contribution to the church was in his strong encouragement of mission:

Reader 2: "Mission is nothing but one church of God in motion."

Reader 1: Loehe preached that the Christian life was a life of love. Thus he and his congregation established a number of social service institutions. He founded a training center for deaconesses and through them he set up a home for the poor, a home for unwed mothers, a home for the emotionally ill, a hospital for men and a hospital for women. No wonder that Loehe came to be called, "the Great Heart of Neuendettelsau."

It was during the same period, the middle of the 1800s, that many Germans were emigrating to America. A German Lutheran pastor in Fort Wayne, Indiana, Fredrich Wyneken, wrote an open letter to the people of Germany asking for help.

Reader 2: "Come now, dear reader, and enter the settlements and log huts of your brethren! Behold now husband, wife and children must work hard to fell the giant trees, to clear the virgin forest, to plow, to sow and to plant, for their pittance of money runs low or is already gone .... But look at their souls — for years they have been without the Word of life, no Table of the Lord has been spread for them. They have grown used to their spiritual death."

Reader 1: Wyneken's letter was published in Germany, and it came to Loehe's attention. He was deeply moved by this opportunity for mission, and he issued an appeal of his own:

Reader 2: "Our brethren are living in the wildernesses of North America — without food for their souls. We sit on our hands and forget to help them ... Shall we simply look on

14

while our brethren in the faith are led astray because of a lack of shepherds, merely observe while the evangelical church in North America disintegrates? Shame on us if we do not do what we can! ... Up, brethren, let us help as much as we are able!''

Reader 1: Loehe followed his strong words with action. He sought volunteers who would be willing to be missionaries to the United States, individuals who had not gone through the traditional German educational system, but yet had a love for the mission of the church. Two young men responded to Loehe's appeal, and they spent a year of training under his supervision. In 1842 these two were commissioned as missionaries and sent to begin their ministry in Ohio. Many more followed them, and they came to be called Loehe's "emergency men." The American Lutheran church relied greatly on these missionaries as German immigrants pushed farther and farther west. Loehe wrote:

Reader 2: "Though we do little, we are doing something ... God can make it bigger!''

Reader 1: Another one of Loehe's missionary experiments was not as successful: the establishment of a whole colony of German immigrants who would work among the native Americans in Michigan. Four of these colonies were founded, Frankenmuth being the largest. The colonies themselves grew and prospered, but their work among the Indians was not very successful and finally failed entirely when the government transferred the Indians to a distant reservation.

Among these German immigrants the issue of language would arise again and again. Loehe himself was a strong proponent of continuing the German language in America:

Reader 2: "When the Englishmen keep their language to themselves they may regard it as lovely as they wish. But when they offer it to us in place of our German tongue, only a man who has never learned to distinguish between a beautiful and an ugly sound would be ready to surrender his beautiful German for the evil-sounding mish-mash.''

Reader 1: Later on Loehe could see the handwriting on the wall, and he admitted:

Reader 2: ''We are far from believing that the German Lutheran Church is to stand or fall with the German language.''

Reader 1: It was more important, he felt . . .

Reader 2: ''. . . to see our brethren more and more returning to the full truth of the Lutheran church and, in another tongue, confess themselves of the same faith and the same hope with us.''

Reader 1: These ''emergency men'' of Loehe had been ordained by the American Lutheran church, and eventually they joined in partnership with a group of Saxon German Lutherans under the leadership of C. F. W. Walther. Together they founded a seminary in Fort Wayne, Indiana, and another one in Saginaw, Michigan. In 1847, they formed a group of congregations, calling it the Missouri Synod.

Not long after, however, a conflict developed between Walther and Loehe, specifically a disagreement over the doctrine of ministry. Does the ministry derive from the congregation, as Walther believed, or does the congregation derive from the ministry, as Loehe maintained. Loehe certainly admitted that the two of them saw things differently, but he did not feel that their differences should lead to a break in unity. After one attempt at reconciliation, Loehe wrote positively of the spirit of brotherly love between himself and Walther:

Reader 2: ''Such a spirit requires no haste to become one in formulas and theses. Hand in hand they go to the school of the Holy Spirit, where they see over the doorway the inscription: 'The longer, the more love; the longer, the greater unity and faithfulness.' "

Reader 1: Loehe believed that it was not necessary for everyone to see everything in just one way. Can't unity be maintained in spite of differences, with the hope that through God's Spirit and God's Word eventually they could come to see more and more alike?

Walther himself, however, believed differently, and the break finally came in Saginaw, Michigan. Rather than transfer the seminary there to the control of the Missouri Synod, Loehe decided to move it to Dubuque, Iowa, where it still exists today as Wartburg Theological Seminary. Because of the break, it was also necessary to establish a new synod, which was called the Iowa Synod. It later became a part of the American Lutheran Church, and now today, the Evangelical Lutheran Church in American.

Loehe, like Walther, was a strongly confessional Lutheran. Yet Loehe believed that there could be a unity in spite of differences. For example, when he wrote his *Three Books about the Church*, he concluded his preface with these words:

Reader 2: "Peace be with those who say Yes! Peace be with those who say No! God's peace be with all! May we all in peace be one — one church, his church!"

Reader 1: Loehe's theology was a simple one: we are all sinners who need God's grace in order to be saved; and, in fact, it is only by God's grace that we come to faith; and it is only as a result of grace and faith that we are able to lead lives of love.

This creed, which he wrote for the order of deaconesses, could serve as a summary of his own faith:

Reader 2: "What do I want? I want to serve. Whom will I serve? The Lord in his suffering and poor. And what is my reward? I serve neither for reward nor thanks but out of thanks and love; my reward is that I may serve ... And what if I grow old in doing it? Then shall my heart flourish as a palm tree, and the Lord will satisfy me with grace and mercy. I shall depart and be anxious for nothing.''

Reader 1: Loehe continued to serve the church and its mission to the world, all from his humble parish in Neuendettelsau. He died, at the age of 64, on January 2, 1872, never having traveled to America, where his influence has been felt so strongly. Upon his tombstone are those familiar words from the Apostles' Creed:

Reader 2: ''I believe in the communion of saints, the forgiveness of sins, the resurrection of the body, and the life everlasting.''

Bibliography

Wilhelm Loehe, *Liturgy for Christian Congregations of the Lutheran Faith* (translated by F. C. Longaker). Newport, Kentucky, 1902.

Wilhelm Loehe, *Seed-Grains of Prayer* (translated by H. A. Weller). Chicago: Wartburg Publishing House.

Wilhelm Loehe, *Three Books about the Church* (translated, edited and with an introduction by James L. Schaaf). Philadelphia: Fortress Press, 1969.

Erich H. Heintzen, *Love Leaves Home: Wilhelm Loehe and the Missouri Synod.* St. Louis: Concordia Publishing House, 1973.

Gerhard Ottersberg, ''Wilhelm Loehe and Wartburg Theological Seminary,'' a lecture on the 100th Anniversary of His Death, April 11, 1972.

Cyril And Methodius
Missionaries To The Slavs

Date: February 14

Text: 1 Corinthians 14:6-12

Hymn Of The Day: "O God Of Light"

Prayer Of The Day:
God of grace and might, we praise you for your servants, Cyril and Methodius, to whom you gave gifts to make the good news known. Raise up, we pray, in every country, heralds and evangelists of your kingdom, so that the world may know the immeasurable riches of our Savior, Jesus Christ our Lord. Amen. (*LBW* 139, p. 37)

Prayers:
In thanksgiving for Cyril and Methodius, who brought the gospel to the Slavic people in their own language, that we too may aid in the efforts of those who speak the good news in many tongues.

Cyril And Methodius

Missionaries To The Slavs

Reader 1: Today we honor two brothers, Cyril and Methodius, saints from the ninth century who were missionaries to the Slavs of Eastern Europe.

Reader 2: But first a brief refresher course in political history might be helpful. Cyril and Methodius were a part of the old Byzantine Empire, with its capital in Constantinople (where Istanbul, Turkey is located today). This Byzantine Empire ruled in the East.

In the West during this ninth century, Charlemagne had established a western or Frankish Empire. In between these two empires — the eastern and the western — lived the Slavic people in Moravia and Bavaria and Dalmatia — the part of the world that is known today as Eastern Europe: Czechoslovakia, Yugoslavia, Bulgaria. These Slavic people served as a kind of buffer zone between the two empires.

Reader 3: Perhaps a quick review of church history is appropriate as well. At about this same time there is a growing rift between the eastern and western church. The eastern church had its headquarters in Constantinople; the western church was centered in Rome.

The Pope is the Bishop of Rome, and during this ninth century was still regarded as the head of the entire Christian Church — eastern and western. But that unity was beginning to show signs of strain.

Several issues of doctrine contributed to that strain. In the eastern church, icons were a valuable part of the worship and devotional life of Christians. In the West they were seen as "graven images" which should be destroyed. That's where we get the term "iconoclast," which means "image-smasher."

Another divisive issue beginning to surface at this time was the "filioque" controversy. "Filioque" is Latin for "and the Son." It refers to that phrase in the third article of the Nicene Creed: "We believe in the Holy Spirit, the Lord, the giver of Life, who proceeds from the Father and the Son."

Talk about a really involved doctrinal dispute! The phrase had not appeared in the original creed in the fourth century, but some of the East wanted to add it. Those in the East were opposed. In the ninth century, the issue was far from settled. Later, it became one of the main issues splitting the Roman Catholic Church in the West from the Orthodox Church in the East.

Reader 1: It was into that mixed political and religious atmosphere that the brothers Cyril and Methodius were born in the early ninth century in Thessalonica, Greece. That made them part of the Byzantine Empire politically and the eastern church religiously. Both boys were students in Constantinople, receiving an education that would prepare them for some government post in the empire. Methodius, in fact, was appointed governor of an outlying district, but later renounced it all to become a monk. His younger brother, Cyril, refused such a government post even at the beginning. Instead, he studied for the Christian ministry, was ordained a deacon, and became chief assistant to the patriarch of Constantinople.

In 862, Prince Rastislav, leader of the Moravian Slavs, asked the Byzantine Emperor:

Reader 4: "Our people has renounced paganism and is observing the Christian law, but we do not have a teacher to

21

explain to us the true Christian faith in our own language in order that other nations, seeing this, may imitate us. Send us therefore, Master, such a bishop and teacher, because from you emanates always to all sides, the good law.''

Reader 1: The Emperor sent Cyril and his brother, Methodius, to the Slavs, to explain the true Christian faith in their own language. Because of the many Slavs living in their boyhood home of Thessalonica, both Cyril and Methodius had grown up speaking the language.

The Slavs had wanted Christianity to be taught to them in their own language, but the problem was that they had no alphabet. That was Cyril's first task: to create a 38-letter alphabet which would be able to convey the unique sounds of the Slavic language. His new alphabet was inspired by Hebrew and Greek, but resulted in a very original and useful alphabet called glagolithic. Perhaps you have seen examples of Russian writing, which uses the Cyrillic alphabet — Cyrillic, named for Cyril, the saint whom we honor today. Early biographies of Cyril stress the fact that God had revealed this new Slavic alphabet to Cyril . . .

Reader 4: ''. . . in order that you too may be counted among the great nations which praise God in their own language.''

Reader 1: Cyril then began teaching his new alphabet to the Slavs and translating the gospels and the liturgies.

Reader 5: You and I may take it for granted that we read the Bible and worship our God in our own language. But back in the ninth century that was not usually the case. Back then it was generally held that there were three sacred languages — Latin, Greek and Hebrew — the three languages which Pilate had used for the inscription above Jesus' cross. There were many in the church who felt that Cyril had gone too far. They complained to the Pope who summoned the two brothers to Rome.

Reader 3: It was a newly elected Pope, Hadrian II, who welcomed Cyril and Methodius in Rome . . . and he welcomed them with open arms. He received the Slavic books which the brothers had translated, blessed them and deposited them in the Church of St. Mary. Furthermore, he arranged to have several Slavic students ordained — and what's more, he allowed their ordination liturgy to be sung in the Slavic language!

Reader 1: Unfortunately, at this same time, Cyril became seriously ill. It was his wish that he die as a monk. When he took his solemn vows as a monk, he is reported to have said:

Reader 4: "From now on I am the servant neither of the emperor nor of anyone on earth, but only of God the Almighty."

Reader 1: Fifty days later, on February 14, 869, Cyril died. He was only 42 years old. His biographer noted that he died with a prayer on his lips, a prayer with three requests: that God would bless his work, that the Slavs might continue to be able to worship in their own language, and that there might be unity in the church.

Reader 5: The very lives of these two brothers are lived-out examples of the unity of the church. They were both raised and trained in the eastern church and yet they recognized the authority of the Pope in the western church and were willing to submit themselves to his authority. The Slavic liturgy which Cyril composed was actually a combination of the Byzantine and Roman liturgical rites. In the midst of a church that was heading toward schism, they were fervently seeking unity.

Reader 1: Following Cyril's death, the Pope consecrated Methodius as an archbishop. He returned to Moravia carrying a papal letter which gave official permission to the Slavs to worship in their own language *(although the Pope requested that the Epistle and the Gospel should first be read in Latin*

23

before being read in the Slavic language). However, Methodius' neighboring bishops did not accept him, this easterner who was given so much authority among western Christians. One of them had Methodius arrested and he was imprisoned in a monastery for 2½ years until finally he was freed through the Pope's intervention.

During his remaining years in Moravia, Methodius and his disciples translated the entire Bible into the Slavic language. In addition his disciples began extending their mission among the Slavic people in Poland and Russia. Methodius himself died 16 years after his brother on April 6, 885.

Reader 5: Unfortunately, a couple of centuries later the great work of Cyril and Methodius was abruptly reversed. In 1074, the Roman Catholic Church forbid the use of any language other than Latin in the Mass. The Slavic people greatly resented this, and it paved the way for an early reformer of the church to arise — the Czech, John Hus. However, the Pope declared Hus' evangelical views heretical and, in 1415, John Hus was burned at the stake.

But a century later, when the German reformation got under way, it was quickly welcomed by the church in Bohemia, Moravia and Slovakia. Once again the Slavic people were able to worship again in their own language.

Bibliography

Francis Cvornik, *Byzantine Missions Among the Slavs.* New Brunswick, New Jersey: Rutgers University Press, 1970.

Jaroslav Pelikan, *The Spirit of Eastern Christendom (600-1700).* Chicago: University of Chicago Press, 1974.

A. A. Skodacek, *Slovak Lutheran Liturgy: Past and Present.* 1968.

Thomas Aquinas:
Teacher Of The Church

Date: March 7

Text: Proverbs 9:1-10

Hymn Of The Day: "Of The Glorious Body Telling" or "Thee We Adore, O Hidden Savior" *(Both hymns were written by Thomas Aquinas.)*

Prayer Of The Day:
Almighty God, your Holy Spirit gives to one the word of wisdom, and to another the word of knowledge, and to another the word of faith. We praise you for the gifts of grace imparted to your servant Thomas Aquinas, and we pray that by his teaching we may be led to a fuller knowledge of the truth which we have seen in your son Jesus Christ our Lord. Amen. *(LBW, 145, p. 38).*

Prayers:
In thanksgiving for Thomas Aquinas, the great teacher of the church, that we may be led by his teaching to praise you for the goodness of creation and to thank you for the even greater goodness of your Word made flesh, Jesus Christ.

Thomas Aquinas

Teacher Of The Church

Reader 1: Was it the greatest of centuries for Christianity? Here are just a few names which might convince us of the glory of the 13th century: Saint Francis of Assisi, Saint Dominic, Albertus Magnus, Roger Bacon, Bonaventure, Dante and Thomas Aquinas.

One of the outstanding achievements of this 13th century was the beginning of a new monastic movement. Led by Saint Dominic and Saint Francis of Assisi, these new friars did not stay within the walls of a wealthy monastery, but rather they traveled the countryside preaching and begging for alms. The great philosopher/theologian Thomas Aquinas eventually became one of these new Dominican monks, but not without a great struggle.

Born in 1224, the youngest son in a noble Italian family, his parents dedicated Thomas to a life of service in the church. But they were thinking along the lines of the more traditional, respectable monasticism — like the Benedictine Abbey of Monte Cassino — which was where Thomas began his training at the age of five.

At 14 he continued his studies at the University of Naples. There he became acquainted with several Dominican monks and eventually decided to become one of them. These Dominicans were a new order of wandering teachers and preachers who had an evangelical zeal for the salvation of souls. Thomas Aquinas later described this new kind of monasticism as the best of all: a contemplative life of study and prayer which went beyond the old monasticism because it shared the fruits of that contemplation with others.

But Thomas' family was horrified at his decision. G. K. Chesterton, a British literary figure from our own century, has wittily described their reactions this way:

Reader 2: "It was as if the eldest son of the squire might go home and airily inform the family that he had married a gypsy."

Reader 1: Thomas' brothers took matters into their own hands and kidnapped him and locked him up in a tower room on the family estate. In their attempts to persuade Thomas to leave the Dominican order, they even used a prostitute! Bernard Gui, a 14th-century biographer, tells the story:

Reader 3: "So a lovely but shameless girl, a very viper in human form, was admitted to the room where Thomas was sitting alone, to corrupt his innocence with wanton words and touches. But if she expected a man, she found an angel ... Chastity and indignation leapt up together. Springing toward the fire that burned in his room, Thomas seized a burning log from it and drove out the temptress, the bearer of the lust's fire. Then, his spirit still aflame, he drew on the wall of the room, with the charred tip of the log, the sign of the holy cross."

Reader 1: Seeing that Thomas was not about to cave into their demands, his family finally relented. Thomas then joined his Dominican brothers in Cologne, where he studied philosophy and theology under another great Dominican, Albertus Magnus. Here Thomas became a part of that 13th-century movement that "rediscovered" Aristotle, the pagan Greek philosopher of the fourth century B.C. These scholars used Aristotle's writing to defend traditional Christian teachings.

27

Thomas Aquinas was an extremely shy and reserved student, speaking very little in class. He was also very large — fat, we might say. So his classmates called him "the dumb ox." But one day he dropped some of his notes and a fellow classmate took them to Albertus Magnus, who realized at once what a brilliant student Thomas Aquinas was. So Thomas was invited to defend a certain proposition in class. Here is Bernard Gui's description of the incident;

Reader 3: "After setting out the arguments for and against the thesis, Thomas then proposed a certain distinction as sufficient to solve the problem and answer the objections: whereupon Master Albert said: 'Thomas, you seem to be not only discussing the question — which is your task — but deciding it too!' Then he began to press Thomas with many strong and, one might have thought, decisive objections; but to each one Thomas had a sufficient answer. And the story goes that at last Albert exclaimed: 'We call this lad a dumb ox, but I tell you that the whole world is going to hear his bellowing!' "

Reader 1: A definitely prophetic remark! The most important of all of Thomas' writings, his *Summa Theologiae,* continues to be the only theological work on virtually every list of great books.

At the end of Thomas' student days, he was ordained to the priesthood and became a lecturer and later a professor at the University of Paris. What was it then that this brilliant teacher passed on to his students?

In his reliance upon Aristotle, Thomas Aquinas was reconciling Christianity with reason and with science. Chesterton wrote:

Reader 2: "Saint Thomas was willing to allow the one truth to be approached by two paths, precisely because he was sure there was only one truth. Because the Faith was the one truth, nothing discovered in nature could ultimately contradict the Faith. Because the Faith was the one truth, nothing really deduced from the Faith could ultimately contradict the facts."

28

Reader 1: Thomas, along with Aristotle, emphasized the importance of the five senses, the human body, the experience of the common person. As Chesterton points out, for too long Christianity had been following Plato with his emphasis on the spirit as opposed to the body. But as Chesterton reminds us, the Body of Christ had hung upon the cross ...

Reader 2: "... It had risen from a tomb. It was no longer possible for the soul to despise the senses ... Plato might despise the flesh; but God had not despised it. The senses had truly become sanctified."

Reader 1: All this, of course, led Thomas to defend the orthodox Christian teaching that God's creation is good. Chesterton again gives us a good summary of Thomas' teaching about creation:

Reader 2: " 'God looked on all things and saw that they were good.' [This] is the thesis that there are no bad things; but only bad uses of things. If you will, there are no bad things, but only bad thoughts; and especially bad intentions."

Reader 1: In all of Thomas' theology there is a strong affirmation of life. Chesterton again:

Reader 2: "The only working word for that ... is Optimism. [Thomas] did, with a most solid and colossal conviction, believe in Life; and in ... the liveableness of life ... If the morbid Renaissance intellectual is supposed to say, 'To be or not to be — that is the question,' then [Thomas] does most certainly reply in a voice of thunder. 'To be — that is the answer.' "

Reader 1: Although most of Thomas' writings are theological and philosophical in nature, he did write a liturgy for the Feast of Corpus Christi, a liturgy specifically celebrating the Real Presence of Christ in the Eucharist. Thomas had always felt that the Eucharist was the most sublime of all the sacraments. Bernard Gui tells us that Thomas, like every priest, celebrated the mass every day and oftentimes ...

Reader 1: "... while saying mass he was utterly absorbed by the mystery, and his face ran with tears."

Reader 1: In our own *Lutheran Book of Worship* we have two hymns written by Thomas Aquinas, both of them Eucharistic hymns: "Of The Glorious Body Telling" and "Thee We Adore, O Hidden Savior." *(This statement can be changed to fit other denominations.)*
If all of this has conveyed something to us about the thought and theology of Thomas Aquinas, what can we say about the man himself? Bernard Gui tells a story which illustrates the humility.

Reader 3: "[Thomas] was in the cloister, walking meditatively around as he was wont to do, when a brother from another priority who did not know him approached and said, 'Good brother, the prior says that you are to come with me.' The prior had in fact given that brother permission to take the first man he should happen to meet as his companion on some business that he had to see to in the city. Thomas bowed his head at once and followed. Now the other was a fast walker, too fast for Thomas, who could not keep up with him and got many hard words in consequence, but each time begged the other's pardon. And this was noticed and wondered at by people in the city; for they recognized the great teacher who was hurrying after that undistinguished friar; and, thinking there must be some mistake, they at last told the latter who his companion was. And he, turning round, then apologized to Thomas, begging him to excuse his ignorance. But Thomas, seeing the people salute him respectfully and hearing them ask why he had let himself be treated in this way, gently pointed out that the way to perfection lies only through obedience; and if God, he said, had humbled himself for our sake, should not we submit to one another for God's sake?"

Reader 1: Thomas' desire was to live simply as a friar. He had no ambitions for higher church office. In fact, he refused several ecclesiastical positions, including that of archbishop of Naples. Once, when his friends jokingly asked him if he would like to be lord of Paris, Thomas replied that he would much rather be able to find a copy of Saint Chrysostum's commentary on the Gospel of Matthew!

As usual, Chesteron very well sums up this attitude of Thomas:

Reader 2: "It is as if Napoleon had insisted on remaining a private soldier all his life."

Reader 1: The stories that tell of Thomas' powers of concentration arc legendary. For example, there is the fact that he could dictate to four secretaries at once, each one taking down notes on a different subject. Or there is the amusing story of Thomas being invited to a banquet where he was sitting next to King Louis IX; lost in thought, he was completely oblivious to the conversations around him. All of a sudden, Thomas brought his fist down on the table and shouted: "That will settle the Manichees!" All the time he had been working on an argument to refute the Manichean heresy that the world is evil.

The end of Thomas' life has an element of mystery to it. After saying mass on December 6, 1273, he never wrote another word. When pressed for an explanation, Thomas confided to his secretary: "All that I have written seems to be like so much straw, compared to what I have seen and what has been revealed to me." He died four months later on March 7, 1274, at the age of 50. He received the Eucharist on his deathbed, and according to his biographer, Bernard Gui, he made the following confession:

Reader 3: "O price of my redemption and food for my pilgrimage, I receive you. For your sake I have studied and toiled and kept vigil. I have preached you and taught you.

Never consciously have I said a word against you. But if I should have said or written anything amiss on this sacrament or any of the others, I leave it all to the judgment of the holy Roman Church, in obedience to whom I desire to end my life."

Bibliography

G. K. Chesterton, *St. Thomas Aquinas,* London: Hodden & Stoughton, 1943.

Bernard Gui, *(Translated by Kenelm Foster) The Life of Saint Thomas Aquinas.* London: Longmans, Green and Co., 1959.

Anthony Kenny, *Aquinas.* New York: Hill and Wang, 1980.

Jaroslav Pelikan, *The Growth of Medieval Theology (600-1300).* Chicago: University of Chicago Press, 1978.

James A. Weisheipl, *Friar Thomas D'Aquino: His Life, Thought, and Works,* Garden City: Doubleday & Company, 1974.

Perpetua And Felicity:
Courageous Martyrs

Date: March 7

Text: Joel 2:28-32

Hymn Of The Day: "O Morning Star, How Fair And Bright, *(especially verses 5 and 6)*

Prayer Of The Day:

Gracious Lord, in every age you have sent men and women who have given their lives for the message of your love. Inspire us with the memory of those martyrs for the gospel, like your servants Perpetua and Felicity, whose faithfulness led them in the way of the cross, and give us courage to bear full witness with our lives to your Son's victory over sin and death; through Jesus Christ our Lord. Amen.

Prayers:

In thankfulness for Perpetua and Felicity and the other martyrs of the church, that their faithful courage may be the seed of faith growing in us.

Perpetua And Felicity

Courageous Martyrs

Reader 2: "The blood of the martyrs is the seed of the church."

Reader 1: So spoke Tertullian, one of the early church fathers. From time to time in the first several centuries of the church's existence, anti-Christian persecution would break out in the Roman Empire. Christians were a favorite target because they refused to make sacrifices for the welfare of the emperor, whom the state regarded as a god.

So it happened with seven young Christians in the African city of Carthage in the year 202. Six were arrested, all of them catechumens who were being prepared for Christian baptism. The seventh person was Saturus, their teacher, their catechist; he had not been with his students when they were arrested, but later turned himself in so that he could share their fate.

Vibia Perpetua was one of those arrested, along with her slave, Felicity. Perpetua kept a journal while she was in prison, as did Saturus, her chatechist. An eyewitness to their deaths as martyrs joined their two written accounts and added an introduction and conclusion of his own.

Some have claimed that this eyewitness/editor was none other than Tertullian, one of the early church fathers. If it were

Tertullian, what an irony that would be! That he would be the one responsible for preserving this beautiful story of courage and love and faithfulness of a Christian woman!

Because, you see, Tertullian was an influential representative of that group of Christian theologians who held a very negative opinion of women. For example: women, through Eve, were the source of sin in the world; according to God's will, women were to be subjected to men; women were not allowed to be teachers in the church.

The story of Perpetua stands out in marked contrast to these theological views. Here is the story of a woman who has much to teach the church: about the struggle to make moral decisions, about courage, about love.

Why did the compiler put this account together? Listen to his own words:

Reader 2: "For this reason we deem it necessary to pass on this written account for the glory of God, lest anyone with a weak or despairing faith might think that supernatural faith prevailed solely among the [biblical] ancients."

Reader 1: The compiler sets the scene:

Reader 2: "Arrested were some young catechumens: Revocatus and Felicitas *(both servants),* Saturninus, Secundulus, and Vibia Perpetua, a young married woman about 20 years of age, of good family and upbringing. She had a father, mother, two brothers (one was a catechumen like herself), and an infant son at the breast. The following account of her martyrdom is her own, a record in her own words of her perceptions of the event."

Reader 1: So let's listen to Perpetua's own story. One of her great difficulties was her relationship with her father, a Roman nobleman and not a Christian himself. Over and over again he attempted to persuade her to make the sacrifice to the emperor and thereby gain her freedom.

35

Reader 3: "While I was still with police authorities my father out of love for me tried to dissuade me from my resolution. 'Father,' I said, 'Do you see here, for example, this vase, or pitcher, or whatever it is?' 'I see it,' he said. 'Can it be named anything else than what it really is?' I asked, and he said, 'No.'

"So I also cannot be called anything else than what I am, a Christian.' For a few days my father stayed away. I thanked the Lord and felt relieved because of my father's absence. At this time we were baptized and the Spirit instructed me not to request anything from the baptismal waters except endurance of physical suffering."

Reader 1: Another of Perpetua's concerns was her infant son. She felt a deep sense of responsibility and love for him. Yet if she maintained her courageous witness to Christian truth, she would lose her life and thus deprive her son of his mother.

Reader 3: "A few days later we were imprisoned. I was terrified because never before had I experienced such darkness. What a terrible day! Because of crowded conditions and rough treatment by the soldiers the heat was unbearable. My condition was aggravated by my anxiety for my baby . . . In my anxiety for my infant I spoke to my mother about him, tried to console my brother, and asked that they care for my son. Then I was granted the privilege of having my son remain with me in prison. Being relieved of my anxiety and concern for the infant, I immediately regained my strength. Suddenly the prison became my palace, and I loved being there rather than any other place."

Reader 1: Then came the day of Perpetua's trial.

Reader 3: "Hilarion, the governor, who assumed power after the death of the proconsul Minusius Timinianus, said, 'Have pity on your father's grey head; have pity on your infant son; offer sacrifice for the emperor's welfare.' But I answered, 'I will not.' Hilarion asked, 'Are you a Christian?' And I answered, 'I am a Christian.' . . . Then the sentence was passed; all of us were condemned to the beasts. We were overjoyed as we went back to the prison cell. Since I was still nursing my child who was ordinarily in the cell with me, I quickly sent the deacon Pomponius to my father's house to ask for the baby, but my father refused to give him up. Then God saw to it that my child no longer needed my nursing, nor were my breasts inflamed. After that I was no longer tortured by my anxiety about my child or by pain in my breasts."

Reader 1: They were "overjoyed" when the sentence was passed. It is difficult for us to take that in. Yet it was considered a privilege to die for the faith. Their martyrdom would be like their second baptism. In fact, if a Christian were martyred before he had been baptized, his death was regarded as a "baptism in blood."

All of which is not to say that Perpetua did not at first fear her confrontation with the wild beasts. But while she was in prison she had several dreams which helped to reassure her and shore up her courage. In one of the dreams she saw a ladder, stretching from earth to heaven. At the top was a beautiful garden. She was climbing this ladder and having to fend off a fierce dragon as she did so. But she reached the top — a symbol of God's kingdom — and a grey-haired man dressed like a shepherd — God, we are to presume — said, "Welcome, my child," and offered her cheese — the heavenly banquet?

Reader 3: "I awoke, still tasting the sweet cheese. I immediately told my brother about the vision, and we both realized that we were to experience the sufferings of martyrdom. From then on we gave up any hope in this world."

Reader 1: Our compiler gives us some further information about Felicity, Perpetua's slave, also arrested.

Reader 2: "As for Felicity, she was too touched by God's grace in the following manner. She was pregnant when she was arrested and was now in her eighth month. As the day of the contest approached, she became very distressed that her martyrdom might be delayed, since the law forbade the execution of a pregnant woman. Then she would later have to shed her holy and innocent blood among common criminals. Her friends in martyrdom were equally sad at the thought of abandoning such a good friend to travel alone on the same road to hope.

"And so, two days before the contest, united in grief they prayed to the Lord. Immediately after the prayers her labor pains began. Because of the additional pain natural of an eighth month delivery, she suffered greatly during the birth, and one of the prison guards taunted her: 'If you're complaining now, what will you do when you're thrown to the wild beasts? You didn't think of them when you refused to sacrifice.' She answered, 'Now it is I who suffer, but then another shall be in me to bear the pain for me, since I am now suffering for him.' "

Reader 1: The compiler does give us the gruesome details of the contest itself. "Contest?" Why do they call it a contest? Pitting human beings against a bear, a leopard and a wild boar is no contest. The seven were finally released from their pain and from their earthly lives by the swords of the gladiators. But ...

Reader 2: "... before doing so the seven kissed each other so that their martyrdom would be completely perfected by the rite of the kiss of peace."

Reader 1: The kiss of peace, which was exchanged in worship on every Lord's day, just before the Eucharist was celebrated, the foretaste of the feast to come. The kiss of peace preparing these young martyrs for the heavenly feast at God's banquet table.

Reader 2: "O brave and fortunate martyrs, truly called and chosen to give honor to our Lord Jesus Christ! And anyone who is elaborating upon, or who reverences or worships that honor, should read these more recent examples, along with the ancient, as sources of encouragement for the Christian community. In this way there will be new examples of courage witnessing to the fact that even in our day the same Holy Spirit is still efficaciously present, along with the all powerful God the Father and Jesus Christ our Lord, to whom there will always be glory and endless power. Amen."

Bibliography

Marie Anne Mayeski, *Women: Models of Liberation.* Kansas City: Sheed & Ward, 1988. [Which contains the full text of the *Passion of Perpetua and Felicity,* reprinted from A Lost Tradition: *Women Writers of the Early Church,* translated by Rosemary Rader, University Press of America, 1981.

Athanasius
Faithful Teacher

Date: May 2

Text: Matthew 22:41-46; 2 Timothy 4:1-7

Psalm: Psalm 136

Hymn Of The Day: "We All Believe In One True God," or "Son Of God, Eternal Savior"

Prayer Of The Day:
Heavenly Father, shepherd of your people, we thank you for your servant, Athanasius, who was faithful in the care and nurture of your flock; and we pray that, following his example and the teaching of his holy life, we may by your grace grow into the full stature of our Lord and Savior Jesus Christ. Amen. (*LBW* 143, p. 38)

Prayers:
In thanksgiving for the life of Athanasius, teacher and defender of the faith, that we too may confess the Christian faith and live in its power.

Athanasius

Faithful Teacher

Reader 1: In the early part of the fourth century it suddenly became a lot less dangerous to be a Christian. Constantine was made Roman Emperor and in 311 he issued an Edict of Toleration. Christians would no longer be persecuted for their faith.

Conflict with the empire had ended, so Christians were now much freer to fight among themselves! There is both cynicism and truth in that statement. The truth is that a certain false belief, a heresy, had crept into the Christian faith, and the church spent the greater part of the fourth century contending against it. Its leader in this struggle was Athanasius, Bishop of Alexandria, Egypt.

Athanasius was born into a Christian family in Egypt in the year 295. Here is a story about his youthful years; and it may be more story than fact, but it does illustrate his early commitment to the Christian faith.

Reader 2: A previous Bishop of Alexandria, whose name was Alexander, was in his home along the seashore. Looking out the window he saw some children playing on the beach. And it appeared to the Bishop that these children were "playing church" — one of them was baptizing the others. Thinking that perhaps the imitation had gone too far, he had the children brought to him and he questioned them. Bishop Alexander discovered that everything had been done in good order, and he decided that the baptisms were official. The name of the young baptizer was Athanasius.

Reader 1: Bishop Alexander encouraged Athanasius to study for the priesthood. Soon he was ordained as a deacon, then archdeacon, becoming very much a valuable assistant to the bishop.

At this time a Christian priest by the name of Arius began to promote his view that the Son of God was not a full and equal partner in the Trinity. In all fairness to Arius, we must admit that his belief was an attempt to solve one of the problems of the Trinity: did Christians believe in just one God or in three gods? Arius tried to save the unity of God by sacrificing the divinity of the Son of God — not a good solution to the problem. This belief of Arius also made God a distant god; oh, yes, this God had a son, but this son was much lower than the Father; the son didn't even fully understand the Father. Arianism became very popular, especially in the East. Even street songs were used to spread its influence among the people.

To Bishop Alexander — and to Athanasius — this was a neresy that must be stamped out. And because this issue threatened to divide the church, Roman Emperor Constantine called a council of the entire church. All bishops were to meet in Nicea *(modern-day Turkey)* in 325 to settle the matter.

Athanasius, even though only an assistant to the bishop, was a major speaker at this Nicene Council. In the end a majority of the bishops took a stand against Arianism, and they developed a creed to express the orthodox faith, the Nicene Creed:

Reader 2: "We believe in one God, the Father, the Almighty, maker of heaven and earth, of all that is, seen and unseen.

We believe in one Lord, Jesus Christ, the only Son of God, eternally begotten of the Father ...."

Reader 1: Are you listening to this, Arius?

Reader 2: "... God from God, Light from Light, true God from true God, begotten, not made, of one Being with the Father ..."

Reader: And if somehow Arius hadn't gotten the message, this was added at the very end:

Reader 2: "And those who say, 'Once he was,' and 'Before his generation he was not,' and 'He came to be from nothing; or those who pretend that the Son of God is 'of other substance or essence' or 'created,' or 'alterable,' or 'mutable,' the Catholic Church anathematizes."

Reader 1: Which means "they curse." And Arius found himself kicked out of the church, excommunicated. However, this was not the end of the controversy, but only the beginning. Athanasius himself would spend the next 50 years of his life battling against this heresy.

Soon thereafter Alexander died and Athanasius was elected Bishop of Alexandria, at the very young age of 33. Almost immediately he was verbally attacked by Arius and his followers. Their accusations were not so much theological — after all, hadn't Roman Emperor Constantine himself supported the theological conclusions of the Nicene Council? Rather, the charges were political. Listen, now, to some of their accusations:

Reader 3: Athanasius levied a tax in Egypt in order to cover church expenses.

Reader 1: Athanasius easily disproved that charge.

Reader 3: Athanasius gave money to an enemy of the empire, a rebel.

Reader 1: Again, the charge was easily disproved.

Reader 3: Athanasius sent a priest into a local church to cause a disturbance while the resident priest was leading the Eucharist.

Reader 1: This charge, too, was disproved.

Reader 3: Then came the charge, the most ludicrous of all, that Athanasius had murdered Arsenius, one of his Egyptian bishops; furthermore, that he had cut off his hand and was using it for magicial purposes!

Reader 1: When Emperor Constantine heard that charge, he summoned Athanasius for trial. In a most dramatic way, Athanasius was able to disprove this charge as well.

Reader 2: Arsenius, of course, had not been murdered, but had only been hidden away by the Arians. At Athanasius' trial the Arians produced a box containing a human hand which they claimed belonged to Arsenius. Meanwhile, Athanasius' supporters had found Arsenius and brought him to the trial wrapped in a cloak. Athanasius paraded the cloaked Arsenius, first revealing his face, then one hand, and then the other; and then Athanasius inquired, "Where did he grow the third hand which you have in the box?"

Reader 1: Those charges, too, were proved to be false. Finally, however, these Arian opponents came up with an accusation that stuck:

Reader 3: Athanasius prevented a shipment of corn from sailing to the Roman capital.

Reader 1: Constantine accepted this charge and he exiled Athanasius to the hinterland of the Empire, to Gaul, which we know now as France. Did Constantine really believe that Athanasius was guilty of this crime, or was he acting to protect Athanasius, to remove him from these Arian opponents and thus save his life? We just don't know for sure. In any case, this was only the first of five exiles that Athanasius would be subjected to in his life.

While in Gaul Athanasius continued his practice of writing an annual Easter letter to the Egyptian churches. Here are some excerpts:

Reader 2: "It is true that I have been hindered by those hardships that you have probably heard about, and several trials have been laid upon me. And we have been separated by a great distance ... Nevertheless, the Lord has strengthened and comforted us in our affliction. So we have not been afraid, even in the midst of such schemes and conspiracies, to send you word about our saving Easter Feast — even from the ends of the earth!

"After all, how can we expect to develop patience if we haven't faced sorrow and hard work? Or how would we ever experience fortitude if our enemies never attacked us? How could we ever show courage if we never had to face bad treatment and injustice?

"Our Lord and Savior Jesus Christ, therefore, is an example to us of how to suffer ... *(As the Apostle Paul has written),* 'I can do all things through Christ who strengthens me *(Philippians 4:13)* and 'In all these things we are conquerors through Christ who loved us' *(Romans 8:37).*"

Reader 1: For the remainder of his life Athanasius would be in and out of favor with the various Roman emperors, depending upon whether they supported the Arian heresy or the orthodox view laid down by the Nicene Council. We need to realize that this was a time of theological fluctuation for the church. It was mainly because of the faithful persistence and courage of Athanasius that the church eventually came to accept the full divinity and power of the Son of God.

Several stories have come down to us which illustrate the faith and determination of this man of God.

Reader 2: Once while Athanasius was conducting worship in an Alexandrian church, Roman soldiers came and surrounded the building. Athanasius very calmly instructed the deacon to lead the congregation in the reading of Psalm 136, a psalm of praise where the congregation's line is repeated in each verse: "for [God's] steadfast love endures forever." Athanasius remained in the church until the people had departed safely, and then he himself was whisked into hiding.

At another time Athanasius was on a boat heading up the Nile, being pursued by another boat full of Roman soldiers. When his boat rounded a bend, Athanasius ordered the captain to turn around and thus to meet his pursuers head on. The leader of the pursuing boat, not recognizing the approaching ship, called out, "Have you any news of Athanasius?" According to the story, Athanasius himself replied, quite truthfully, "He is not far off," and the government boat passed without further incident!

Reader 1: Certainly Athanasius' influence was felt in other aspects of the church's life as well. During an exile in Rome, Athanasius became close to Pope Julius and convinced him of the value of the monastic life of the Egyptian desert monks. Thus Athanasius, an eastern church leader, came to be regarded as the father of western monasticism.

Nor is it difficult for us to see the influence of Athanasius even in our time. The Nicene Creed, with its forceful statements about the full divinity of Jesus Christ, the Son of God, is one of the foundations of our faith and worship life today. It is a statement of the church's belief that our God is not a distant God, but that God took on human flesh and became one of us. It is a reminder to us that God is near, that God's creation is good, that our humanity has value and worth.

46

Athanasius is also a model and example of faithfulness for us. He was determined that the Arian heresy would not triumph. And, in fact, he was willing to endure exile and suffering to see that it would not prevail. These words from the Second Letter to Timothy could very well have been spoken by Athanasius: "I have fought the good fight and I have finished the race, I have kept the faith (2 Timothy 4:7)."

Bibliography

William Bright, *Lessons from the Lives of Three Great Fathers,* London: Longmans, Green & Co., 1890.

Lynn Harold Hough, *Athanasius: the Hero,* Cincinnati: Jennings and Graham, 1906.

Jaroslav Pelikan, *The Emergence of the Catholic Tradition (100-600)*, Chicago: University of Chicago Press, 1971.

Jack N. Sparks, *The Resurrection Letters,* Nashville: Thomas Nelson Publishers, 1979.

Ludwig Nommensen
Missionary To The Bataks

Date: May 23

Text: Matthew 4:18-22

Hymn Of The Day: "Before You, Lord, We Bow"

Prayer Of The Day:
God of grace and might, we praise you for your servant, Ludwig Nommensen, to whom you gave gifts to make the good news known. Raise up, we pray, in every county, heralds and evangelists of your kingdom, so that the world may know the immeasurable riches of our Savior, Jesus Christ our Lord. Amen. *(LBW* 139, p. 37)

Prayers:
In thanksgiving for the life and ministry of Ludwig Nommensen, missionary to the Bataks, that his patience and courage in sharing the good news may inspire our witness in this day.

Ludwig Nommensen

Missionary To The Bataks

Reader 1: In the Pacific Ocean of southeastern Asia lies the country known as Indonesia. You may remember some of the Indonesian islands from your geography class back in grade school: Borneo, Java, Sumatra.

It is on the island of Sumatra, specifically the northern part, where the Batak people live. For centuries the Bataks lived in isolation from the world; not too many foreigners wanted to penetrate that mountainous tropical jungle region. As far back as Marco Polo, the Batak people were characterized as fierce and cannibalistic. Even the Dutch colonialists were only able to dominate the coastal areas. Nor had Hindus, Buddhists and Muslims made any inroads among the Batak people.

With that kind of isolation from the world, the Bataks had their own very well developed society: a system of laws, social customs and religion. According to the Batak worldview, all existence was divided into three realms: first, the Upper World which was the domain of the High God and the spirits of the departed ancestors; second the Middle World, or the earth, where humans lived; third the Under World which was the home of ghosts and demons.

The Bataks were not afraid of their gods; once they even declared war on them! According to another religious tradition,

49

one of their gods came down to earth but decided that the problems of the middle world were too difficult and so he left, never to return!

A very different kind of morality resulted from this religious worldview. To enter the kingdom of the dead, a Batak would be asked how many heads he had taken; the more, the better. Thus a murderer could enter the kingdom of the dead, but not his victim.

They believed that each person possessed a tondi, a life force, the essential power of a person. They further believed that one could absorb the power of another person's tondi by eating him; thus they practiced cannibalism.

So how would you go about introducing Christianity to the Batak people? On the one hand, you wouldn't want to weaken the very strong society they had developed; but on the other hand, you wouldn't want Christianity to be totally transformed by their culture.

In 1834, two American missionaries, Henry Lyman and Samuel Munson, made the first attempt to travel into the interior of Sumatra to the Batak people. They were surrounded by 200 armed men, killed and supposedly eaten.

In that same year, 1834, Ludwig Nommensen was born on one of the islands off the coast of the Netherlands. When he was 12 years old, he was run over by a farm wagon, injuring his legs so severely that it was thought he would never walk again. Lying in bed for a year, young Ludwig prayed for healing. Then a new doctor prescribed a different treatment and soon Nommensen was walking again. This healing, Nommensen believed, was God leading him to become a missionary. As a young adult he sought admission to a missionary training school in Barmen. At first glance his application was rejected, but Nommensen's persistence finally gained him entrance. He graduated in 1861, was ordained and sailed for Sumatra. He spent the first two years living on the coast and learning the Batak language, because he intended to begin his ministry among them.

Finally, accompanied by two Batak guides, he journeyed into the interior. His arrival in a Batak village caused quite a stir; no one there had ever seen a white man before. He was taken to the radja, the leader of the village, where he made his request:

Reader 2: "I would like very much to come and live with you here in order to teach all who wish to, how to become clever and happy."

Reader 1: The men of the village debated his request for a whole day. Unable to reach a decision, the radjas from the nearby villages were invited for a conference. The arguing went on for five days. Finally, the radjas allowed him to stay. But his attempts to establish himself there were continually frustrated. He lived in a rice barn because the people did not allow him to erect a building. He tried to start a school, but no children would attend.

Once, at a feast, to honor one of their ancestors, a medium had incited the crowd to demand Nommensen's death. Nommensen boldly stood in their midst. The medium fell silent at his feet as soon as he began to speak.

Reader 2: "Men of Sitahoeri, you have been deceived because the spirit which spoke through the medium just now was a lying spirit, Satan himself, and not the spirit of Siatasbaritas, your ancestor. Would he have asked you for human blood as an offering? No, this is Satan, the great deceiver who makes people murder each other. But God, the Creator, has sent me here to you in order to show you the deception of the Evil One and to lead you in the way of salvation."

Reader 1: Nommensen's speech calmed the crowd, and he was allowed to leave unharmed. There were many such difficulties in the early days. The mission work went slowly; after two years he had baptized only 13 Batak people.

51

Yet increasingly, Nommensen came to understand the unique Batak logic and began winning their confidence. He lived as simply as the Bataks did: he slept on a mat on the floor, used a box for his chair and a sack of rice for his table. His daily food was the same as theirs: a bowl of rice, a piece of dried fish and maybe a vegetable.

The first converts to Christianity found themselves banished from their villages, so Nommensen established a Christian community on a piece of swampland. He called it Huta Dame, or Village of Peace. During a smallpox epidemic many of the surrounding villages brought their children to Nommensen for treatment.

In spite of the initial slow progress of the mission, Nommensen patiently continued sharing the gospel. His watchword was "tole," which in the Batak language means, "onward."

One of his early converts was a radja, Pontas Lumbantobing. One day this radja led Nommensen to the top of a small hill, took his hand in his and said to him:

Reader 3: "When you first came to us you could hardly find a place to build a house, for we did not welcome you and you had to settle at Huta Dame. You know it is not healthy there because of the frequent floods and the dampness. You, sir, have been sick unto death ... Not long ago you told us the story of the great King who said, 'Friend, go up higher.' Now the little radja says to you, 'Sir, go up higher.' Break down your house at Huta Dame and rebuild it here. Radja Pontas gives you this place."

Reader 1: Radja Pontas' gift was a major step forward for the Christian mission among the Batak. Nommensen continued to share the Gospel of Jesus Christ, weaving it into the very fabric of their social customs. He established medical centers and introduced better agricultural techniques. Nommensen believed that gospel ministry and social ministry were equally important.

Reader 2: "For when the spiritual message has been accepted, the people become more conscious of the social misery in which they have been living."

Reader 1: Nommensen's greatest accomplishment was his insistence upon training the Batak people to become pastors. In 1882 he established a seminary and soon Bataks were preaching the gospel to Bataks. Nommensen had a dream of what the Batak church could become. He wrote this in a letter to the mission center at Barmen:

Reader 2: "In spirit I see scattered everywhere Christian congregations, schools and churches, groups of Bataks old land young, making their way to these churches; on every side I hear the sound of church bells calling the believers to the house of God. I see everywhere cultivated fields and gardens, green pastures and forests, tidy villages and dwellings in which are found properly dressed descendants of this people. Still more, I see preachers and teachers, natives of Sumatra, standing on the platforms and behind the pulpits, pointing out the way of the Christian life to both young and old. You will say that I am a dreamer, but I say, No! I am not dreaming. My faith visions all this; it shall come to pass for all kingdoms shall be his and every tongue confess that Christ is Lord to the glory of God the Father. Therefore, I am encouraged, though the people may oppose me and make all sorts of plans to resist God's word, they can just as easily keep the ocean back from its shores as to keep God's word from their hearts. A stream of blessing shall certainly flow over them. Already the day begins to appear. Soon the clear light will break forth and then shall the Sun of Righteousness in all his glory shine over the horizon of Batakland from the South even to the shores of the Toba Sea."

Reader 1: Nommensen was able to see his dream come true. Once the Batak people themselves had been trained to be pastors and teachers, the church grew by leaps and bounds.

When Nommensen had begun his work among the Bataks, it was their strong family ties and sense of corporate identity that made those earlier conversions so difficult. Now it was those same solid family ties which converted whole villages to Christianity. Recalling Jesus' words about making his disciples "fishers of men," Nommensen remarked:

Reader 2: "Now it was their task not to fish with a hook, but with a net."

Reader 1: When Nommensen died in 1918, the Batak Protestant Church had 180,000 baptized members. In 1970 there were 2,000,000 Batak Christians.

Much of the fantastic growth of the Batak Christian church is due to the patient faithfulness and courage of Ludwig Nommensen and especially his emphasis upon a Batak church for a Batak people. The Batak church now has missionaries of its own, all over Indonesia, and even in other parts of the world:

Reader 3: "It is commonly said that where you find one Christian Batak there is a man who talks about his faith; where there are two there is a prayer meeting; where there are three you find a church — and with four a choir. The little congregation of 20 Bataks in New York City supports this saying."

Bibliography

Nellie DeWaard, *Pioneer in Sumatra,* London: China Inland Mission, 1962.

Paul B. Pedersen, *Batak Blood and Protestant Soul,* Grand Rapids, Michigan: Wm. Eerdmans, 1970.

Ph. Lumban Tobig, *The Structure of the Toba-Batak Belief in the High God,* Translated by C. A. Eijken and J. Twigt, Amsterdam: Jacob Van Campen, 1956.

The Rule Of
Saint Benedict

Date: July 11

Text: Psalm 1

Hymn Of The Day: "Rise Up, O Saints Of God"

Prayer Of The Day:
O God of wisdom, in your goodness you provide faithful teachers for your church. By your Holy Spirit give all teachers insight into your Word, holy lives as examples to us all, and the courage to know and do the truth; through your Son, Jesus Christ, our Lord. Amen. *(LBW* 198, p. 46)

Prayers:
For Saint Benedict, whose rule has guided so many Christian communities in 1,500 years, that he and his rule may also be a guide for us, pointing us to God and the coming kingdom.

Saint Benedict

The Rule Of Saint Benedict

Reader 1: You are driving along Interstate 94, just west of St. Cloud, Minnesota. All of a sudden you see, rising out of the trees in the distance, the large concrete banner of the chapel at Saint John's Abbey in Collegeville. If you entered this Benedictine monastery at the right time of day, you could see the monks, dressed in their cowls, processing in for worship.

Or maybe you are exploring the countryside around Dubuque, Iowa, and there in the midst of the rolling hills is a Trappist monastery, Our Lady of New Melleray.

Monasteries — they seem so anchored in another century, and yet they still are signs of the church, signs of faithfulness and vitality even in this 20th century. How did it all begin, this urge to separate oneself from the world?

The Christians of the first and second centuries found themselves automatically separated from the world, oftentimes by bloody persecutions. But that all changed in the fourth century when Roman Emperor Constantine officially recognized Christianity. Certainly at first these warmer relations between church and state were much preferred over the previous oppression. But when the Roman Empire itself began to decline, Christians were again reminded that the kingdom of God was not of this world.

Several of the early church fathers, like Antony the Great, became hermits in the Egyptian desert. Of course, there were very few who could endure the harshness and loneliness of that extreme separation from the world. But what about a community of people who would live separately from the world? Saint Benedict was not the first to establish such communities, but his rules for that kind of monastic living have endured even to this day.

We know about Saint Benedict's life mainly through an account written by Pope Gregory the Great. Benedict was born in 480 into an Italian Christian family. As a young man he was sent to Rome to complete his education but very quickly became disenchanted with "the ways of the world." As Pope Gregory wrote:

Reader 2: "In his desire to please God alone, he turned his back on further studies, gave up home and inheritance and resolved to embrace the religious life."

Reader 1: He eventually spent three years living as a hermit in a cave, growing in faith and struggling with personal temptations. For example, Gregory tells this story of Benedict's battle with lust. He was remembering a woman he had once seen and his sinful thoughts were running wild.

Reader 2: "Almost overcome in the struggle, he was on the point of abandoning the lonely wilderness when suddenly with the help of God's grace he came to himself. He then noticed a thick patch of nettles and briars next to him. Throwing his garment aside he flung himself into the sharp thorns and stinging nettles. There he rolled and tossed until his whole body was in pain and covered with blood. Yet, once he had conquered pleasure through suffering, his torn and bleeding skin served to drain the poison of temptations from his body."

Reader 1: I think most of us today would be quite skeptical about Benedict's solution to the temptations of lust. Yet as Pope Gregory tells us:

Reader 2: "He never experienced another temptation of this kind."

Reader 1: Primitive electric shock treatment, we might call it. But many men attached themselves to Benedict to learn from him. He left his hermitage and established several monastaries for these followers of his. And in order to guide their life together in community, he wrote his famous rules for monastic living.

Reader 3: "Listen, my son, and with your heart hear the principles of your Master. Readily accept and faithfully follow the advice of a loving Father, so that through the labors of obedience you may return to him from whom you have withdrawn because of the laziness of disobedience (Prologue)."

Reader 1: It would be hard to miss Benedict's main theme: obedience. Not exactly a popular virtue today, is it? We in the 20th century tend to value independence over obedience.

Perhaps here is also a good place for us to raise an objection to the very premise of monasticism: that it is a way to grow closer to God through good works. Benedict states this very clearly:

Reader 3: "If we wish to be sheltered in [God's] kingdom, it can be reached only through our good conduct (Prologue)."

Reader 1: What about Martin Luther's experience in the monastery? Didn't his attempts to earn his salvation lead only to despair? Benedict does emphasize the Christian cooperating with God's grace to lead the sanctified life, to produce these good works. Lutherans would probably want to stress God's grace more and our cooperation less. *(Lutherans may add the next sentence.)* But also let's not forget our own Lutheran Confessions and their insistence that "good works are necessary."

Luther, of course, realized that one can never do enough if your aim is to please God through your good works; one is always going to fall short. Benedict, too, was well aware of human sin and failure. So when he lists 72 tools of good works, he saves the most important for last:

Reader 3: "Never despair of God's mercy (Chapter 4)."

Reader 1: The real key in Benedict's ordering of monastic life was the abbot, the head of the monastery. The word "abbot" comes from the Hebrew word for father, "Abba."

Reader 3: "He is Christ's representative ... He should show the sternness of a master and the love and affection of a father ... The abbot shall not make distinctions among the people in the monastery. No one shall be loved more than the others, except those who are found more obedient or observant in his faith (Chapter 2)."

Reader 1: There's that all-important virtue again: obedience. Another trait which Benedict sought to develop in himself and in his monks was humility.

Reader 3: "Therefore, brothers, if we wish to reach the highest peak of humility and soon arrive at the heavenly height, we must, by our good deeds, set up a ladder like Jacob ... we go up by humbling ourselves and down by praising ourselves (Chapter 7)."

Reader 1: That, too, grates against many Protestant sensitivities, doesn't it — that we arrive in heaven because of our good deeds and humility? Perhaps Benedict would have done better to remain faithful to the biblical story of Jacob's ladder. In Jacob's dream the ladder is not a way for him to climb up to God, but rather it's a way for God to climb down to Jacob! Another biblical reminder of God's grace.

Perhaps Benedict's most lasting contribution to the monastic life was his concern for the individual monk and his natural weaknesses. The Rules are characterized by simple common sense. For example, Benedict laid out the usual Sunday morning liturgy, but made this exception:

Reader 3: "The only exception is if the monks — Heaven forbid — arise late; then the lessons or responses may be shortened a bit (Chapter 11)."

Reader 1: An individual monk would not be counted as tardy for worship unless he arrived after the gloria of Psalm 95; and Benedict very charitably stipulated:

Reader: "... and on account of this the psalm should be chanted slowly (Chapter 43)."

Reader 1: Now there's a gospel orientation for you! There is a punishment for coming late, but if you sing the Gloria slowly, no one has to be punished!
Benedict determined that the monks would chant all 150 psalms during a week's worth of worship, which at times seemed excessive to the monks, but Benedict reminded them:

Reader 3: "Our spiritual fathers performed with determination in one day what we now take a whole week to do (Chapter 18)."

Reader 1: What was life like in one of Benedict's monasteries? Each day revolved around worship, communal work and study. Eight times a day the community gathered together for worship: 2 a.m., 4 a.m., 6 a.m., 9 a.m., 12 noon, 3 p.m., 6 p.m. and 8 p.m.
Food at the monastery was very simple:

Reader 3: "We believe that two cooked dishes will satisfy the daily needs at each meal ... if some brothers cannot eat one, then they may eat the other ... A third dish may appear if fresh fruit or vegetables are available ... A pound of bread will be allotted to each monk daily ... Except for the sick, no one is to eat meat (Chapter 39)."

Reader 1: And to drink:

Reader 3: "One-quarter liter of wine for each monk each day is adequate we believe ... We read that wine is not for monks, but in our times they cannot accept this. Let us therefore agree on this limit at least, lest we satiate ourselves with drink (Chapter 40)."

Reader 1: During each meal, a reader would read from the writings of the church fathers.

Reader 3: "No whispering or noise is to be heard, only the voice of the reader. The brothers should hand around food and drink so that no [verbal] request is needed (Chapter 38)."

Reader 1: As for clothing ...

Reader 3: "Suitable clothes shall be given the monks, dependent on the climate ... Each monk will make do with a cowl and tunic — heavy for winter, light for summer. He shall also have a shift for labor and shoes for the feet. Monks should not complain of the color or texture of their clothes. It shall be whatever is available in the surrounding countryside or whatever is cheapest (Chapter 55)."

Reader 1: All of this may seem harsh compared to our modern lifestyles. But we should realize what life was like in Benedict's day, especially in the fifth century when the Roman Empire was disintegrating. A typical peasant would be lucky to get one meal a day and most likely would not even have a change of clothing. In addition, there was always the threat of invasion and war.

All of these regulations for the monastic life were set down in a book which became known as *The Rule Of Saint Benedict*. It was quickly adopted by a number of monasteries, and by the ninth and tenth centuries it was made the rule for all monastic communities. In fact, down through the years, whenever there is an attempt to bring reform to monastic life, it is almost always done by returning to *The Rule Of Saint Benedict.*

That is even true for the amazing reform which has swept through almost all western monastic communities since the Second Vatican Council. Sister Joan Chittister, a Benedictine Prioress in Erie, Pennsylvania, believes that the entire *Rule Of Saint Benedict* is summarized in just one section toward the end, titled, "The Good Zeal Monks Should Possess."

It's almost as if he says, "Now don't get carried away with this thing. Holiness can be destructive. Sanctity can be an evil zeal."

And what is the right kind of zeal?

Reader 3: "monks should practice this zeal with ardent love . . . accept each other's frailties . . . try to outdo each other in obedience . . . Let no one do what is best for himself, but rather what is best for another."

Reader 1: In other words, it is a rule of love. And when, in your natural human frailty, you have failed in loving, remember also that God is love and therefore . . .

Reader 3: ". . . never despair of God's mercy."

Bibliography

Joan D. Chittister, *Living the Rule Today,* Erie, Pennsylvania: Benet Press, 1982.

Anthony C. Meisel & M. L. del Mastro (translators), *The Rule Of Saint Benedict,* New York: Doubleday, 1975.

Odo John Zimmerman (translator), *The Fathers of the Church: St. Gregory the Great: Dialogues* (Volume 39), New York: Fathers of the Church, 1959.

Bartolome' de Las Casas
Protector Of The Indians

Date: July 17

Text: Luke 9:51-56 [*This preface could be read before the reading of the gospel:* "Bartolome' de Las Casas was an early American priest who was given the title, 'Universal Protector of the Indians.' He spoke out unceasingly against the Spanish conquerors of America who were intent upon destroying the native peoples. In support of his protection of the Indians, Las Casas often referred to this story from the Gospel of Luke:"]

Hymn Of The Day: "In Christ There Is No East Or West" *(with non-sexist changes in the third verse)*

Prayer Of The Day:
   O God, you made us in your own image and redeemed us through Jesus your Son. Look with compassion on the whole human family; take away the arrogance and hatred which infect our hearts; break down the walls that separate us; unite us in bonds of love ; and, through our struggle and confusion, work to accomplish your purposes on earth; that, in your good time; all nations and races may serve you in harmony around your heavenly throne; through Jesus Christ our Lord. Amen. (*LBW* 177, p. 44)

Prayers:

For Bartolome' de Las Casas, Protector of the Indians, that we may be led by his life and example to see all people as children of God, who are therefore our brothers and sisters.

Bartolome' de Las Casas

Protector Of The Indians

Reader 1: In 1992, North, Central and South Americans celebrated the 500th anniversary of Columbus' "discovery" of America. Of course, we have been reminded that it can't really be called a "discovery" when there were people already living here who knew this land existed all the time!

So what's a better word? "Exploration?" Perhaps most fitting is the word "conquest." After 1492, as the Spaniards established their American empire, 20,000,000 native Americans were killed. In some areas, like Cuba, all of the native people were destroyed. The conquistadors would surround a village, imprison all the inhabitants in a large house, then set fire to it. Or they would loose their ferocious dogs among the natives, and they would be mauled to death.

European diseases were also a factor in the deaths of so many Americans, but perhaps the single greatest cause was slavery. And it happened at the very beginning. Christopher Columbus gave each one of his returning men an Indian as a slave. Isabella, Queen of Spain, when she heard what Columbus had done, remarked:

Reader 2: "Who gave permission to Columbus to parcel out my vassals to anybody?"

Reader 1: The Spanish crown did object to outright slavery, so the conquerors had to devise a way of doing it legally. Columbus himself suggested the system of "repartimientos" or "parceling out" — the process whereby the natives were to be parceled out among the Spaniards to do work in the mines, the pearl fisheries and the farms. As Columbus wrote to King Ferdinand and Queen Isabella:

Reader 2: "May it please Your Majesties to allow that these Indians may be made use of, for a year or two, until this business of colonization be placed on a good footing."

Reader 1: The system was approved and it existed for much longer than just "a year or two." It later came to be called "encomienda" or "recommendation" — a more pleasing name, but still a euphemism for slavery.

Bartolome' de Las Casas was born in Spain in 1474, and as a young adult found himself on the receiving end of that system. His own father had sailed with Columbus; and after Bartolome' graduated from the university with a law degree, he sailed for America in 1502 to seek his fortune. He took up farming and mining in Hispaniola, now called the Dominican Republic — certainly not that he himself farmed or mined, but rather he benefited from the forced labor of the natives.

However, over the next several years Las Casas became convinced of the injustice of the "encomienda" system. Perhaps it was a sermon by that Dominican friar, Montesimos, that persuaded him:

Reader 2: "I ascended this pulpit to let you know that I am the voice of Christ crying in the wilderness of this island. Hence it is meet that you listen to it with no ordinary attention, but with all the power of your souls and of your five senses. It will prove to you the strongest, the most rasping, the harshest, the most frightful voice you ever listened to. This voice tells you that all of you are now living and dying in a state of mortal sin, on account of your cruelty and tyranny over these innocent people. Tell me: with what right and with what justice do you subject the Indians to so cruel and to so horrible a slavery? With what authority do you wage your abominable wars against these people, who were living peaceably in their own countries, where you cause infinite numbers of them to die by your unheard of barbarities and slaughter? Why do you overwhelm them with work, and give them no sufficient food to keep them from starving or medicines to cure their infirmities? Nay, why do you kill them daily with excessive labor that they may bring you gold? What steps have you taken to have them taught to know God, their Creator, to be baptized, to hear mass and to keep the Sundays and Holy Days? Are you not bound to love them as yourselves? Have you lost your reason, have you lost your senses? Or are you buried in a lethargic sleep?''

Reader 1: It was through the influence of these Dominican preachers that Las Casas himself became a priest in 1510, the very first to be ordained in America. Early on he began working for the abolition of Indian slavery in the Americas. On his first assignment as a parish priest in Cuba, he witnessed the massacre of an entire Indian village of 2,000 inhabitants. When it was all over, the captain proudly asked Las Casas: "Father, what do you think of the work of these our Spaniards?" His reply:

Reader 3: "I commend them to your care and to that of the devil."

Reader 1: The abuses which Las Casas witnessed daily were so great that he decided to sail home to Spain to inform King Ferdinand of what was actually happening. Las Casas had a friend in the royal court who arranged for him to speak to the king. Ferdinand was receptive, but unfortunately he died a few days later and the new emperor, Charles V, would not see Las Casas.

However, there were two Spanish cardinals who very strongly agreed with Las Casas, and they sent him back to America with the title, "Universal Protector of the Indians."

His title meant nothing to the Spanish conquistadors back in America. Las Casas found his ministry among the native people continually frustrated by the oppression under which they were forced to live. Many of the natives believed that the Spaniards worshiped gold as their god; and, in light of the first commandment, their assumption was probably correct. One native of Nicaragua commented:

Reader 2: "What is a Christian, what are Christians? They ask for maize, for honey, for cotton, for women, for gold, for silver; Christians will not work, they are liars, gamblers, perverse, and they swear."

Reader 1: Las Casas decided to return to Spain to make his case before the Emperor Charles V. In his audience before the king, he made this plea:

Reader 3: "In order that the glad tidings of Redemption might reach those vast transatlantic regions, the Indians were entrusted to our care. But alas! the damnable Encomiendas choke the voice of the apostles and stop the work of God. For how shall the preacher instruct a people oppressed and broken down by labor? The Spaniards possessed of Encomiendas are the greatest enemies of these apostolic clergymen, who are engaged in the evangelization of the Indians. They fear that if their bondsmen are taught to know the difference between virtue and vice, they will also learn how deficient is the former and how abundant is the latter in their masters. The Indians, they think, hate us now, but they will look upon us as devils incarnate if they learn the Christian religion."

Reader 1: Las Casas asked and received permission from the emperor to set up an experimental colony where he could put into practice an evangelism based upon love, not force. He was assigned to an area along the coast of Venezuela.

But when Las Casas returned to America to set up this Christian colony, he received no support from the American governors. In fact, one of them had just led an expedition into that area, killing and terrorizing the Indians everywhere. Las Casas' experiment was never given a chance to succeed.

In 1523, Las Casas decided to become a Dominican monk — partly out of frustration, but also because the Dominicans supported his strong views against the enslavement of Indians. Eventually he was assigned to Nicaragua and Guatemala where he was able to put his ideas into practice — and they worked! Free from oppression and cruelty whole villages were baptized and became Christian. On one occasion the sermons of Las Casas persuaded an entire company of soldiers to refuse to obey the orders of their captain to go out on an expedition against the Indians.

Later in his life Las Casas wrote a history of the American conquest, titling it, *The Destruction of the Indies.* Drawing upon his 40 years of ministry in the New World, he described in detail the atrocities of the conquerors; yet he admitted:

Reader 3: "To tell all that was done in these provinces would be difficult and impossible to tell and painful to listen to . . . Of all these horrors one could make a thick book that would terrify the world."

Reader 1: His main argument, as always, was a more loving approach to evangelism:

Reader 3: "To kill the Indians to save their souls, or to massacre a certain number of them in order to convert the rest is a gross sin. God does not wish a gain at the price of so great a loss."

Reader 1: This book of Las Casas', plus his many appeals to the Emperor, finally led to the new laws of 1542 which prohibited Indian slavery in the Americas. Making laws, however, is one thing; enforcing them is another.

Las Casas, at the age of 70, was made bishop of Chiapa, a poor diocese in the northern part of Guatemala. There he refused absolution to all of the Spanish slaveowners and refused to admit them to holy communion until they freed their slaves. The Spaniards accused Las Casas of being a Lutheran!

In 1550, Las Casas was called back to Spain to appear once again before the Emperor to answer these charges. It was arranged as a debate between him and Sepulveda, a well-known scholar who supported the right of Spaniards to enslave the Indians. Sepulveda appealed to Aristotle's doctrine of natural slavery, that one part of humanity is designated by nature to be slaves for the other part. He also quoted scriptures, especially Jesus' Parable of the Great Banquet where the banquet host "compelled the people to come in," maintaining that the Spanish crown should force the Indians to become Christians.

Las Casas spent five days responding to Sepulveda's arguments. Among other things, Las Casas argued that it was in dying and not in killing that the apostles had spread the gospel. In the end the view of Las Casas prevailed, and Charles V tightened up the laws against Indian slavery.

Las Casas appears to be quite the hero, doesn't he? And yet he, too, had feet of clay. Early on in his crusade to abolish Indian slavery, Las Casas proposed instead that the Spanish crown should import black Africans to work as slaves in the Americas. In fact, some historians have called Las Casas "the Father of Negro Slavery in America." How could he speak so passionately on behalf of the Indians and yet be so blinded in the matter of black slavery? Even at the age of 70, when he returned to America as bishop, he brought along with him four black slaves. It was only later that he came to see the folly of any kind of slavery:

Reader 3: "I would not now give that advice for the whole world; and ever since I have believed that it is as unjust to enslave Negroes as it is to enslave Indians, and for the same reasons."

Reader 1: Las Casas spent his remaining years in Spain and died at the age of 92. His last will and testament summarized his life and ministry:

Reader 3: "As God is my witness . . . I declare it to be my conviction and faith . . . that, by all the theft, all the deaths, and all the confiscation of estates and other incalculable riches, by the dethroning of rulers with unspeakable cruelty, the perfect and immaculate law of Jesus Christ, and the natural law itself have been broken, the name of Our Lord and of his holy religion have been outraged, the spreading of the faith has been retarded, and irreparable harm done to those innocent people . . . It is now 70 years since we began to scandalize, to rob and to murder those peoples, but, to this day, we have not yet come to realize that so many scandals, so much injustice, so many thefts, so many massacres, so much slavery, and the depopulation of so many provinces, which have disgraced our holy religion, are sins or injustices at all."

Reader 1: Las Casas is still honored today in Guatemala where his image appears on the one-centavos piece, a reminder of his role as "The Universal Protector of the Indians."

Bibliography

Marcel Brion, *Bartolome' de Las Casas,* New York: E. P. Dutton & Co., 1929.

L. A. Dutto, *The Life of Bartolome de Las Casas,* St. Louis: E. Herder, 1902.

Lewis Hanke, *Aristotle and the American Indians,* Chicago: Henry Regney Company, 1959.

Albert Schweitzer
Humanitarian

Date: September 4

Text: Mark 8:34-38

Hymn Of The Day: "O God, Whose Will Is Life And Good"

Prayer Of The Day:
Lord God, your Son came among us to serve and not to be served, and to give his life for the world. Lead us, like your servant, Albert Schweitzer, to serve all those to whom the world offers no comfort and little help. Through us give hope to the hopeless, love to the unloved, peace to the troubled and rest to the weary; through your Son, Jesus Christ, our Lord. Amen. (*LBW* 141, p. 37)

Prayers:
In thankfulness for your servant, Albert Schweitzer, who lost his life in order to save it.

Albert Schweitzer

Humanitarian

Reader 1: He was called "the world's greatest living human being." By the age of 30 he was recognized as a brilliant theologian and acclaimed as an organ virtuoso and interpreter of Bach. But the real greatness of Albert Schweitzer did not lie in any of those accomplishments but rather in his decision to give up those promising careers and become a medical doctor in the jungles of Africa.

In 1875, Albert Schweitzer was born in a Lutheran parsonage in Alsace, the territory that bounced back and forth between French and German control, depending on who had won the most recent war. His childhood was a happy one, except for school. Albert was a dreamer, and he and school simply did not get along.

His love of the out-of-doors helped him to settle on an early career goal: to be the village swineherd so he could roam the lovely Alsatian hills with his pigs. His bedtime prayers always included his own extra petition "for all things that have breath." Later in his life he would write:

Reader 2: "Even when I was a child I was like a person in an ecstasy in the presence of nature without anyone suspecting it. I consider nature as the great consoler. In her I always found calm and serenity again when I was disturbed. And this has only become accentuated during the course of my life . . . Unforgettable pictures of the country are engraved on my memory. I roam among these memories as in a gallery in which are hung the most beautiful landscapes painted by the greatest masters . . . It is said I am a man of action. But at bottom I am a dreamer, and it is in reveries, reviving the living contact with nature, that I gather the powers that make me an active being.''

Reader 1: Also developing in Schweitzer was a sensitivity for the weak and the oppressed. During a friendly wrestling match with a bigger boy, Schweitzer was able to pin his opponent to the ground. But the defeated boy said accusingly, ''Yes, if I got broth to eat twice a week, as you do, I'd be as strong as you are.'' A reminder to the sensitive Albert that not all people were as well off as he.

Life in the parsonage was filled with music; both his father and his mother played the piano. Even at the age of five young Albert was able to improvise his own harmonies to the tunes of his favorite songs and hymns.

When Schweitzer was 14 an amazing transformation occurred in his school work. Between Christmas and Easter that year he moved from the bottom of his class to somewhere near the top — all because of the influence of one inspiring teacher.

It was almost as if a creative talent were bursting out in all directions. His proficiency at the piano and organ also increased tremendously at this time. Almost everything he touched turned to gold. There was a real delight and exhilaration about life in Schweitzer's teenage years, but along with it came a sense of debt. The greater his happiness the more he felt that he owed somebody something in return for it.

He continued his studies at the University of Strasbourg, with an emphasis in theology and philosophy. There he joined a student association which raised money from the rich and every week distributed it among the poor of the community. One day he met an elderly woman who had no mattress to sleep on. Immediately Schweitzer went to his room, picked up his own mattress and delivered it to her home. It was also at this time that Schweitzer developed his lifelong habit of traveling fourth class — the lowest form of railroad accommodations.

He continued to struggle with his sense of debt, this idea that he owed something for the great satisfaction that life brought him. One hot summer day he attended a mission lecture which had as its theme the notion of debt or expiation. Later Schweitzer wrote:

Reader 2: "It was there that I was struck for the first time by this idea of expiation. It had an extraordinary effect on me. Till then, in Dogmatics and New Testament commentaries, this word "expiation" had seemed heavy to handle — it had to struggle to explain why Jesus died for the world's sins. Everything we had hitherto been told was lifeless and petrified, and we noticed in the way the lecturers spoke of it that they seemed ill at ease and were none too clear about it themselves. But now, launched as an appeal to work under the banner of Jesus, this word took on life. It was a cry, a shock, something which sank into you and took hold of you — and as that day ended I understood Christianity better, and I knew why missionary work was needed."

Reader 1: A few months later Schweitzer made a momentous decision. It was in 1896, he was 21 years old, and he awoke one beautiful spring morning with the strong conviction that this debt must be repaid.

Reader 2: "Proceeding to think the matter out at once with calm deliberation, while the birds were singing outside, I settled with myself before I got up, that I would consider myself justified in living till I was 30 for science and art, in order to devote myself from that time forward to the direct service of humanity. Many a time already had I tried to settle what meaning lay hidden for me in the saying of Jesus 'Whosoever would save his life shall lose it, and whosoever shall lose his life for my sake and the gospels shall save it!' Now the answer was found. In addition to the outward, I now had the inward happiness.''

Reader 1: During the next nine years, before he turned 30, Schweitzer made a name for himself as an outstanding theologian. His unique approach was to emphasize the importance of eschatology in Jesus' teaching, especially the importance of the coming of the kingdom of God. For example, Schweitzer pointed out that the Eucharist was more than just a remembering meal; it was an anticipation of the kingdom, "a foretaste of the feast to come."

Schweitzer's theology, it must be admitted, was definitely of the liberal variety. His most famous work, *The Quest for the Historical Jesus,* concluded that it was impossible to discover the Jesus of history; centuries of dogma and doctrine about Jesus had wiped out any trace of the historical Jesus. When the book was published in 1906, it aroused an intense debate among theologians.

Yet it was the spirit of Jesus which guided Schweitzer throughout his life. Certainly many of us would want to claim much more about this Jesus than Schweitzer did, but few of us could claim to follow this Jesus as Schweitzer himself did.

Schweitzer was ordained into the Lutheran ministry in 1900 and became assistant pastor of Saint Nicholas Church in Strasbourg. At one point Schweitzer was criticized for the brevity of his sermons and the senior pastor talked to him about it.

Reader 2: "He was much embarrassed as I was. When he asked what he was to reply to the aggrieved member of the congregation, I replied that he might say that I was only a poor Curate who stopped speaking when he found he had nothing more to say about the text. Thereupon he dismissed me with a mild reprimand, and an admonition not to preach for less than 20 minutes."

Reader 1: During this time Schweitzer was also teaching theology as well as developing his skills as an organist. He made impassioned pleas for the preservation of old tracker organs, many of which were being converted to the newer electropneumatic technology. The tracker organ, which was entirely mechanical, allowed for greater interpretation and sensitivity on the part of the organist. He wrote:

Reader 2: "With the tracker the finger feels a certain tension exactly when the tone comes; it feels the contact point. And the depressed key pushes up under the finger, in order that when the finger shows the slightest impulse to leave it, it may immediately rise with its own strength and lift the finger up with it. The strength of the keys cooperate with the will! With the tracker even the mediocre organist cannot smear. With pneumatics there is no such cooperation on the part of the keys. It makes the playing worse instead of better, and brings to light the slightest fault. Only with the tracker does one come into really intimate relationship with one's organ. In pneumatics one communicates with one's instrument by telegraph."

Reader 1: As his 30th birthday approached, Schweitzer carried out the decision he made nine years earlier. He resigned his position as professor and entered medical school. He would become a doctor and begin a medical mission in Gabon, at that time the northern province of the African Congo. In a sermon preached that year, he took as his text the story of Peter walking across the water towards his Lord who had said to him, "Come," Schweitzer preached:

Reader 2: "Do not stay where you are, but move ahead, move towards Jesus! ... Do not ask yourself whether the road is firm or practicable, fit for the man who follows his inclinations, but look only to see that it is really the road that leads straight to Jesus."

Reader 1: In a letter to a friend, he explained his decision to leave everything to become a medical missionary:

Reader 2: "Now we sit here and study theology, and then compete for the best ecclesiastical posts, write thick learned books in order to become professors of theology . . . and what is going on out there where the honor and the name of Jesus are at stake, does not concern us at all. And I am supposed to devote my life to making ever fresh critical discoveries, that I might become famous as a theologian, and go on training pastors who will also sit at home and will not have the right to send them out to this vital work. I cannot do so. For years I have turned these matters over in my mind, this way and that. At last it became clear to me that this isn't my life. I want to be a simple human being, doing something small in the spirit of Jesus."

Reader 1: Schweitzer completed his medical degree and left for Africa on Good Friday, 1913. His first act upon arriving in Africa was to befriend a horse. Two men were beating their horse, trying to get it to pull a cart stuck in the mud. Schweitzer had them get down from the cart and into the mud where they pushed from behind.

Schweitzer decided to found his medical mission in Lambarene. Soon the indigenous people were coming from miles around to be treated for various diseases: malaria, sleeping sickness, leprosy, tuberculosis and hernias. The following passage written by Schweitzer illustrates the work of his mission:

Reader 2: "[The Africans] also suffer much oftener than white people from strangulated hernia, in which the intestine becomes constricted and blocked, so that it can no longer empty itself. It then becomes enormously inflated by the gases which form, and this causes terrible pain. Then after several days of torture, death takes place, unless the intestine can be got back through the rupture into the abdomen . . . There are few Negroes who have not as boys seen some man rolling in the sand of his hut and howling with agony till death came to release him. So now, the moment a man feels that his rupture is a strangulated one, he begs his friends to put him in a canoe and bring him to me.

"How can I describe my feelings when a poor fellow is brought to me in this condition? I am the only person within hundreds of miles who can help him. Because I am here and am supplied by my friends with the necessary means, he can be saved, like those who came before him in the same condition and those who will come after him in the same condition, while otherwise he would have fallen a victim to the torture. This does not mean merely that I can save his life. We must all die. But that I can save him from days of torture, that is what I feel as my great and ever new privilege. Pain is a more terrible lord of mankind than even death himself.

"So, when the poor, moaning creature comes, I lay my hand on his forehead and say to him: 'Don't be afraid! In an hour's time you shall be put to sleep and when you wake you won't feel any more pain.'

". . . The operation is finished, and in the hardly lighted dormitory, I watch for the sick man's awakening. Scarcely has he recovered consciousness when he stares about him and ejaculates again and again: 'I've no more pain! I've no more pain!' His hand feels for mine and will not let it go. Then I begin to tell him and the others who are in the room that it is the Lord Jesus who has told the doctor and his wife to come to the Ogowe, and that white people in Europe give them the money to live here and cure the sick Negroes. Then I have to answer questions as to who those white people are, where they live, and how they know that the natives suffer so much from sickness. The African sun is shining through the coffee bushes into the dark shed, but we, black and white, sit side by side and feel that we know by experience the meaning of the words: 'And all ye are brothers.' Would that my generous friends in Europe could come out here and live through one such hour!"

Reader: It was there in Africa that Schweitzer developed his life's philosophy which he called simply, "Reverence for Life." It was a solidarity with all living things, an awareness, as he put it, that ...

Reader 2: "... I am life, that wills to live, in the midst of life that wills to live."

Reader 1: Yet, of course, life itself demands death. When young pelicans were brought into the mission to be cared for by Schweitzer, fish needed to be caught to feed them. In order to preserve life, we must destroy life. Schweitzer's point was that we should be aware of this, that our living depends upon the death of other living things. If we are conscious of the price that is constantly being paid for our own living, then we should become increasingly aware of the value of our life.

It wasn't too long before the world bestowed many honors upon Albert Schweitzer. In 1926, he was awarded the Universal Order of Human Merit at Geneva, the Goethe Prize in 1927, culminating in the Nobel Peace Prize in 1953. For Schweitzer his life was simply a living out of his philosophy:

Reader 2: "I am simply a man who does what is natural. The natural thing however, is loving-kindness."

Reader 1: He lived in simplicity. He owned only one necktie, a tie that had been handed down to him from his father. One woman remarked to him, "I know men who have a hundred ties!" Schweitzer replied:

Reader 2: "Really? For one neck?"

Reader 1: Schweitzer described his philosophy of simplicity in a sermon which he had preached back in 1905:

Reader 2: "To content oneself with becoming small; that is the only salvation and liberation. To work in the world as such asking nothing of it, or of men, not even recognition, that is true happiness ... There are things which one cannot do without Jesus. Without him one cannot attain to that higher innocence — unless we look to him in the disappointments of life, and seek in him the strength to be childlike and small in that higher sense."

Reader 1: Schweitzer dragged his feet when it came to modern technology. He detested the automobile, but eventually realized they were necessary and a truck was purchased for the hospital. Yet no one could fail to notice his glee when one lunch hour he announced at the hospital:

Reader 2: "The 20th century has finally arrived here. There are only two motor vehicles in the district, and today the inevitable happened. They collided. We have patched up the drivers. Anyone who feels reverence for machinery is welcome to look after the vehicles."

Reader: In the 1950s, Albert Schweitzer began to speak out against the nuclear testing that was being done by the United States, Britain and the Soviet Union, and the subsequent increase in levels of radioactivity from those nuclear tests. From Oslo, Norway, where he had received the Nobel Peace Prize, Schweitzer issued his "Declaration of Conscience," calling upon all nations to ban nuclear tests.

Schweitzer died at the age of 90, in 1965, having had his coffin made the previous year. The week before he died he was still strong enough to take a last tour of the orchard at Lambarene. A friend described it as follows: "His last walk was wonderful. Once more he passed through the orchard suppported by his cane. He identified every tree he had planted, praised them for their sturdy growth and for their beauty. From the top of the hill he looked over the hospital and was very happy about it."

On his many fund-raising tours of Europe, Albert Schweitzer would speak to large crowds. Invariably, he would begin his speech this way:

Reader 2: "People often ask me, why did you go to Africa? *[Pause]* Because my Master told me to."

Bibliography

James Brabazon, *Albert Schweitzer,* New York: G. P. Putnam's Sons, 1975.

Albert Schweitzer, *My Life and Thought,* London: George Allen & Unwin Ltd., 1933.

Dag Hammarskjold

Peacemaker — A Liturgy

Date: September 18

The Entrance Rite

The Prelude

The Opening Plainsong *(Solo Voice):* "Grant Peace, We Pray, In Mercy, Lord."

Hymn: "God The Omnipotent"

The Greeting:

> P: Grace to you and peace from God the Father and our Lord Jesus Christ. The Lord be with you.

> C: **And also with you.**

The Theme Of The Day

Reader 1: Dag Hammarskjold died _____ years ago today — September 18, 1961. At the time of his death he had been Secretary General of the United Nations for eight years. He died in a mysterious plane crash in the African jungle. Sabotage? Shot down by one of the warring factions in the

Belgian Congo crisis? No one knows. He had gone there to mediate a cease-fire. Two days after his death, the cease-fire was achieved.

The entire world mourned his death. It seemed that everyone had known and heard of the public Dag Hammarskjold — the peacemaker, the negotiator, the mediator. The whole world had followed his peacemaking triumphs.

For example, when China refused to release the dozen American airmen who had been shot down in the Korean War, Hammarskjold personally went to China to negotiate their release. But his efforts at first produced no results. As a part of the diplomacy, the Chinese asked Dag what he would like for his birthday. "Most of all, release of the airmen," was the reply. Two days after his birthday, they were released.

In November of 1956, the Suez Canal crisis leapt into the headlines. It was Dag Hammarskjold who engineered the cease-fire.

Everyone knew the public Dag Hammarskjold. But it was only after his death that the world became aware of the private Dag Hammarskjold — his inner life, the Christian motivation which moved him to commit his life working for world peace. He kept a diary which was discovered only after his death. Scattered throughout our worship this morning various selections from his diary will be read. He himself called this diary "roadmarkers" or "sign-posts." The published version is titled *Markings*. In his own words:

Reader 2: "It's a diary . . . a sort of 'white book' concerning my negotiations with myself — and with God."

Reader 3: "These notes? They were signposts you began to set up after you had reached a point where you had needed them, a fixed point that was on no account to be lost sight of. And so they have remained. But your life has changed, and now you reckon with possible readers, even, perhaps, hope for them. Still, perhaps it may be of interest to somebody to learn about a path about which the traveler who was committed to it did not wish to speak while he was alive. Perhaps — but only if what you write has an honesty with no trace of vanity or self-regard."

Reader 1: Today is a day for contemplation . . . for meditation. A day to hear from a peacemaker who gave his life for the cause of peace. A day for each of us to hear the call of the peacemakers. "Blessed are the peacemakers, for they shall be called children of God."

Before we continue our liturgy with the Confession and Forgiveness, we hear Dag Hammarskjold speak of God's amazing gift of forgiveness.

The Readings From *Markings*

Reader 3: "Forgiveness breaks the chain of casuality because he who ' forgives' you — out of love — takes upon himself the consequences of what you have done. Forgiveness, therefore, always entails a sacrifice. The price you must pay for your own liberation through another's sacrifice is that you in turn must be willing to liberate in the same way, irrespective of the consequences to yourself."

Reader 2: "Forgiveness is the answer to the child's dream of a miracle by which what is broken is made whole again, what is soiled is again made clean. The dream explains why we need to be forgiven, and why we must forgive. In the presence of God, nothing stands between him and us — we are forgiven. But we cannot feel his presence if anything is allowed to stand between ourselves and others."

The Confession and Forgiveness *(Adapted from Nuclear Issues Committee, Edina Community Lutheran Church)*

P: Lord, we say "In you we trust" but in deed it is our weaponry, the works of our hands, that we trust for salvation. So we pray: "Lord, have mercy."

C: **Lord, have mercy.**

P: Christ, we confess our deep hatred and fear of our enemies that blinds us to our own prideful hardness of heart.
We confess that we have rejected the cross you embraced, and with the sword you told us to put away we
have chosen to protect our wealth and power before the
world's suffering millions. So we pray:

C: **Christ, have mercy.**

P: Listen! Here is good news from the lips of our Lord:
"Peace I leave with you; my peace I give to you; not
as the world gives do I give to you." Listen to him, for
through him his Father says, "You are accepted; you
are forgiven; my peace I give to you."

The Readings From *Markings*

Reader 3: "Have mercy
Upon us.
Have mercy
Upon our efforts,
That we
Before Thee,
In love and in faith,
Righteousness and humility,
May follow Thee,
With self-denial, steadfastness and courage.
And meet Thee
In the silence."

Reader 2: "Give us
A pure heart
That we may see Thee,
A humble heart
That we may hear Thee,
A heart of love
That we may serve Thee

A heart of faith
that we may love Thee.

Thou
Whom I do not know
But Whose I am.

Thou
Whom I do not comprehend
But Who hast dedicated me
To my fate.
Thou.

The Kyrie

P: In peace, let us pray to the Lord.

C: Lord, have mercy.

P: For the peace from above, and for our salvation, let us pray to the Lord.

C: Lord, have mercy.

P: For the peace of the whole world, for the well-being of the Church of God, and for the unity of all, let us pray to the Lord.

C: Lord, have mercy.

P: For this holy house, and for all who offer here their worship and praise, let us pray to the Lord.

C: Lord, have mercy.

P: Help, save, comfort and defend us, gracious Lord.

C: Amen.

The Hymn of Praise: *(Tune: Amazing Grace; by Jose Rechlein)*

Amazing grace, the peace of God!
O gift to hear the call
To bring our world the hope of Christ,
The Spirit in us all.

Great God of Peace, Creator God,
Your living Word you give.
"For all your children and yourselves,
Choose life, that all might live!"

O Spirit, come to fill our hearts
That war and hate shall cease;
Renew the earth and make us one,
A Pentecost of peace!

The Prayer of the Day: *(said in unison)*

C: **Lord, make us instruments of your peace.**
Where there is hatred, let us sow love;
Where there is injury, pardon;
Where there is discord, union.
Where there is doubt, faith;
Where there is despair, hope;
Where there is darkness, light;
Where there is sadness, joy.
Grant that we may not so much seek
To be consoled, as to console;
To be understood as to understand;
To be loved as to love.
For it is in giving that we receive;
It is in pardoning that we are pardoned;
It is in dying that we are born to eternal life.

The Liturgy Of The Word

The Lessons: Isaiah 2:1-4 and Luke 19:41-44

The Hymn: "God Of Grace And God Of Glory"

The Paradox Of Being A Peacemaker

Reader 1: When we commit ourselves to the task of being peacemakers, there is a paradox which we must face sooner or later. It is the paradox of affirming life, on the one hand —

88

your own life, the lives of all around you, an abhorrence of killing. And yet, on the other hand, the paradox involves a willingness, a commitment to give your life for peace.

Not to kill for peace, but a willingness to be killed for peace.

Reader 3: "The meaningfulness of death . . . the meaninglessness of killing."

Reader 2: "Do not seek death. Death will find you. But seek the road which makes death a fulfillment."

Reader 1: That paradox was experienced not only by Dag Hammarskjold. Mahatma Gandhi lived and died that paradox. Jesus Christ lived and died that paradox; and it is the resurrection of Jesus Christ which empowers us to live and die that paradox.

The Readings From *Markings* *(with silence between each)*

Reader 1: Here now this potpourri of readings from Hammarskjold's book, *Markings*. Use the silence between each of them to meditate on their meaning for your life.

Reader 2: "I don't know Who — or what — put the question, I don't know when it was put. I don't even remember answering. But at some moment I did answer Yes to Someone — or Something — and from that hour I was certain that existence is meaningful and that, therefore, my life, in self-surrender, had a goal.

"From that moment I have known what it means 'not to look back,' and 'to take no thought for the morrow.'

"As I continued along the Way, I learned, step by step, word by word, that behind every saying in the gospels stands one man and one man's experience. Also behind the prayer that the cup might pass from him and his promise to drink it. Also behind each of the words from the cross."

(Silence for meditation)

89

Reader 3: "For all that has been — Thanks!
For all that shall be — Yes!"

(Silence for meditation)

Reader 2: "To be free, to be able to stand up and leave everything behind — without looking back. To say Yes."

(Silence for meditation)

Reader 3: "Not I, but God in me."

(Silence for meditation)

Reader 2: "I am the vessel. The drink is God's. And God is the thirsty one."

(Silence for meditation)

The Hymn Of The Day: "They Cast Their Nets"

The Prayer Of Dag Hammarskjold *(Markings)*

Reader 3: Thou who art over us,
Thou who art one of us,
Thou who art . . .
Also within us,
May all see thee — in me also,
May I prepare the way for Thee,
May I thank thee for all that shall fall to my lot,
May I also not forget the needs of others,
Keep me in thy love
As thou wouldst that all should be kept in mine.
May everything in this my being be directed to
thy glory
And may I never despair.
For I am under thy hand,
And in thee is all power and goodness.

Give me a pure heart — that I may see thee,
A humble heart — that I may hear thee,
A heart of love — that I may serve thee,
A heart of faith — that I may abide in thee.

The Prayers Of The People

The Prayer of Dag Hammarskjold

Reader 2: Hallowed be thy name, not mine,
Thy kingdom come, not mine.
Thy will be done, not mine,
Give us peace with thee, peace with all people,
    peace with ourselves,
And free us from all fear.

The Lord's Prayer

The Liturgy Of The Eucharistic Meal

The Sharing Of The Peace

The Offertory

The Offertory Response: "Lord, Receive This Company"

The Prayer Over The Gifts

The Words Of Institution

The Distribution

The Concluding Prayer

The Recessional Hymn: "Rise Up, O Saints Of God"

The Benediction

The Postlude

Bibliography

Dag Hammarskjold, *Markings,* (translated by Leif Sjoberg and W. H. Auden), New York: Alfred Knopf, 1964.

Brian Urquhart, *Hammarskjold,* New York: Alfred A. Knopf, 1972.

Saint Ignatius
Eager Martyr

Date: October 17

Text: Romans 8:31-39

Hymn Of The Day: "Faith Of Our Fathers"

Prayer Of The Day:
Almighty God, you have raised up faithful bishops and leaders of your church. May the memory of their lives be a source of joy for us and a bulwark of our faith, so that we may serve you and confess your name before the world; through your son, Jesus Christ our Lord. Amen.

Prayers:
In thankfulness for Saint Ignatius, one who was carried by God and one who carried God to others, that he might be an example for us of faithfulness in a time of trial.

Saint Ignatius

Eager Martyr

Reader 1: In the early years of the second century — sometime around 110 A.D. — a small band of Roman soldiers led a group of prisoners across Asia Minor, through the area which we now know as Turkey. They had begun their journey in Antioch, Syria, and they were on their way to Rome.

One of the prisoners was Ignatius, bishop of the Christian church in Antioch. So young was the Antioch church that Ignatius was only the second bishop to lead the Christians in that city. We don't know the exact reasons for Ignatius' arrest, but it was definitely a part of the persecution against Christians during the reign of the Roman emperor Trajan. Ignatius' eventual destination was the large coliseum in Rome where he would face the wild beasts. To most Romans he would simply be another man condemned to death for their sporting pleasure; to Christians he would be a martyr.

During the six-week journey from Antioch to Rome, Ignatius wrote seven letters to various Christian churches in cities along the way. Our second speaker will be sharing excerpts from these seven letters, beginning with this one to the church at Tralles:

Reader 2: "Ignatius, who is also Theophorus, to her that is beloved by God, the Father of Jesus Christ, to the holy church which is at Tralles in Asia, elect and worthy of God, having peace in flesh and spirit through the power of Jesus Christ, who is our hope through the resurrection unto him; which church I salute in the fullness of God, after the Apostolic manner, and bid her heartiest greeting (Trallians, Introduction).''

Reader 1: Ignatius writes ''after the apostolic manner.'' Of course, the apostle we are reminded of is none other than Paul, who just 60 years earlier had walked some of these same roads in Asia Minor and had also written letters to young Christian churches. Even the problems these two men faced were similar.

For example, Paul wrote about the struggle in the Antioch church between Jewish Christians and Gentile Christians. In his letter to the Galatians, Paul maintained that it was not necessary to be circumcised in order to become a Christian: ''We are not justified by works of the law, but through faith in Jesus Christ (Galatians 2:16).''

Sixty years later Bishop Ignatius was still dealing with those same tensions in the Antioch church.

Reader 2: ''Be not deceived by strange doctrines nor by ancient fables, seeing that they are profitless. For if, until now, we live after the rule of Judaism, we confess that we have not received grace (Magnesians 8).''

Reader 1: From these letters of Ignatius we get a hint of another heresy that had been troubling the church at Antioch: Docetism. The Docetists believed that Jesus did not actually take on human flesh, but that he only ''seemed'' to be a human being. Thus their name, Docetists, from the Greek word for ''seeming.'' For example, they believed that Jesus did not really suffer and die, he only ''seemed'' to. Ignatius was determined to refute this Docetic heresy.

Reader 2: ''Jesus endured all these sufferings for our sake. And he truly suffered, as also he truly raised himself up. Nor is it the case, as some unbelievers affirm, that he only 'seemed'

95

to suffer — rather, it is they who just 'seem' to be ... refusing to confess that he has borne our flesh (Smyrna 2, 5)."

Reader 1: Ignatius stood firm on the orthodox middle ground between these two heresies: the Judaizers on the right, the Docetists on the left. The tension in the Antioch church deteriorated to the point where these dissenting factions would not even celebrate the Eucharist together. Over and over again in his letters, Ignatius would appeal for unity:

Reader 2: "Therefore give heed to keep one Eucharist. For there is one flesh of our Lord Jesus Christ, and one cup in union with his blood (Philadelphians, 4)."

Reader 1: It may have been the conflict between these two groups that led to Ignatius' arrest. Perhaps the controversy became so vocal that it threatened political stability, and so the Roman governor arrested Ignatius. Maybe one of the dissenting groups, seeking to remove Ignatius from the scene, betrayed him to the authorities. In any case, the strife in the Antioch Church was definitely serious.

How could Ignatius reestablish unity in the church? There were no commonly accepted creeds among the Christian churches; that would come 200 years later with the Nicene Creed. Nor was there even a commonly accepted Christian scripture, not yet a New Testament which was universally recognized.

In the absence of creeds or New Testament scriptures, Ignatius appealed to a unity symbolized by the office of the bishop.

Reader 2: "Avoid division; it is the beginning of evil. Follow, all of you, the bishop, as Jesus Christ followed the Father; and follow the presbytery as the apostles. Moreover, reverence the deacons as the commandment of God ... Let no one do anything pertaining to the church apart from the bishop. Let that eucharist be considered valid which is under the bishop or him to whom he commits it. Wherever the bishop is, there let the church be, even as wherever Christ Jesus is, there is the Catholic Church (Smyrna 8)."

Reader 1: Did you catch that? For Ignatius, the unity of the church was symbolized in a three-fold ordering of the ministry: first, the bishop, who had the overall responsibility for the church is given geographical area; second, the presbyters, or pastors, who conducted worship in the various house churches; third, the deacons who carried out the teaching ministry of the church. It is interesting that the 1982 ecumenical statement, *Baptism, Eucharist, and Ministry,* emphasized a similar order of ministry.

Yet Ignatius' appeal for unity was grounded in something more than just the authority of the clergy. A much stronger basis for unity was the shared worship life of the people.

Reader 2: "But in common let there be one prayer, one supplication, one mind, one hope ... Gather yourselves together, all of you, as to one shrine, one God, as to one altar, even one Jesus Christ (Magnesians 7)."

"Share one another's toil, contend together, run together, suffer together, alike in rest and rising be together, as stewards and fellow workers and ministers of God (Polycarp 6)."

"Form yourselves one and all into a choir, that blending in concord, taking the keynote of God, you may sing in unison with one voice through Jesus Christ to the Father ... Therefore it is profitable for you to live in unblameable unity (Ephesians 4)."

Reader 1: The Eucharist especially was a sign of the unity of the church:

Reader 2: "Meet in common assembly in grace, every one of you, one by one, in one faith and in one Jesus Christ ... breaking one bread, which is the medicine of immortality, the antidote preserving us that we should not die but live forever in Jesus Christ (Ephesians 20)."

Reader 1: One could read these letters of Ignatius and almost forget the terrible death that was waiting for him in Rome ... almost, but not quite. Certainly for Ignatius himself, thoughts of his impending martrydom were a constant companion. It was a martyrdom which he eagerly embraced.

Reader 2: "Why then have I wholly given myself up to death, to fire, to the sword, to wild beasts? Because he that is near to the sword is near to God, he that is in the presence of wild beasts is in the presence of God. Only it is in the name of Jesus Christ that I endure everything, that I may suffer with him (Smyrna 4)."

Reader 1: In his letter to the church at Rome, Ignatius appeals to them not to intercede with the authorities on his behalf.

Reader 2: "I write to all the churches, and charge them to know that I die willingly for God, if you do not interfere. I entreat you, do not befriend me. Allow me to belong to the wild beasts, through whom I may attain unto God. I am God's grain, and I am ground by the teeth of wild beasts, that I may be found to be pure bread of Christ (Romans 4)."

Reader 1: We who are so far removed from such persecution may want to criticize Ignatius for being almost obsessive about his martyrdom.

Reader 2: "I long for the beasts that are prepared for me. I pray too that they may do their work quickly. I will even tease them so that they devour me promptly (Romans 5)."

Reader 1: And yet if you or I were facing such a horrible death, would we not obsess about it, too? But the fact of the matter is, for you and me, in this time and place, there is no possibility of martyrdom. Ignatius could have addressed these words to us:

Reader 2: "I am a condemned man, you have obtained mercy; I stand in danger, you are safely established (Ephesians 12)."

Reader 1: Every Sunday we pray as Ignatius would have prayed, "Save us from the time of trial." That is, "Keep us faithful to you, Lord God, especially when we are tempted to fall away from you." Ignatius remained faithful to the end; he was mauled to death by the wild animals in the Roman coliseum.

As with many martyrs, fanciful legends came to be told about Ignatius. As we noted from his letters, he liked to call himself Theophorus, which can mean, "the one who is carried by God." Thus developed the legend that Ignatius was the little child whom Jesus scooped up in his arms, according to Mark 9:36-37.

A second legend derives from the other sense of that name, Theophorus: "God-bearer." Vincent of Beauvais writes: "When the heart of Ignatius was cut into small pieces by the wild beasts, the name of the Lord Jesus Christ was found inscribed in golden letters in every single piece; for he had said that he had Christ in his heart."

The details of the legends are indeed fanciful, but behind the legends stands a truth; Ignatius was Theophorus, God-bearer and one carried by God.

Bibliography

Virginia Corwin, *St. Ignatius and Christianity in Antioch,* New York: Yale University Press, 1960.

J. H. Strawley (translator), *The Epistles of St. Ignatius,* London: Society for Promoting Christian Knowledge, 1935.

Joel David Wenger, *The Moment to Attain God,* M.A. Thesis, Luther Northwestern Theological Seminary, St. Paul, Minnesota, 1990.

John Christian Frederick Heyer
First American Lutheran Missionary

Date: November 7

Text: Jonah 3:2 *(John Christian Frederick Heyer, missionary to India, was the first to be sent by American Lutherans. This brief passage was the text for the sermon preached at his commissioning service on October 5, 1841.)*

Hymn Of The Day: "O Zion, Haste, Your Mission High Fulfilling"

Prayer Of The Day:
God of grace and might, we praise you for your servant, John Christian Frederick Heyer, to whom you gave gifts to make the good news known. Raise up, we pray, in every country, heralds and evangelists of your kingdom, so that the world may know the immeasurable riches of our Savior, Jesus Christ our Lord. Amen. (*LBW* 139, p. 37)

Prayers:
In thanksgiving for your servant, John Christian Frederick Heyer, that we too may spread the good news of Jesus Christ both here at home and throughout the world.

John Christian Frederick Heyer

First American Lutheran Missionary

Reader 1: The year is 1869. A group of Lutheran pastors and laypersons had come together for a convention in Reading, Pennsylvania. A 77-year-old man, his long white hair curling up at the ends, rises to speak to the assembly. He argues passionately for the Lutheran church to resume its missionary work in India.

The speaker is John Christian Frederick Heyer, who 27 years earlier had been American's first Lutheran foreign missionary. He had been sent twice as a missionary to India, so he definitely knew what he was talking about. But could he do more than just talk about it? Listen to his own words:

Reader 2: "Although I am nearly 77 now, I am willing to go to India myself and reorganize that work!"

Reader 1: The assembly is astounded. A delegate jumps to his feet and asks, "Will Pastor Heyer tell us how soon that will be?" Heyer reaches down to the floor, picks up his suitcase and holds it up for everyone to see and replies:

Reader 2: "I am ready now!"

Reader 1: John Christian Frederick Heyer was born in Helmstadt, Germany in 1793. Almost immediately after his confirmation in the Lutheran Church at the age of 14, he set sail for America, specifically the city of Philadelphia, where his uncle took him on as an apprentice in the furrier trade.

Heyer learned quickly how to make the beaver hats which were so popular in that day. He joined Zion Lutheran Church, a German-speaking congregation; he sang in the choir, attended a Bible study group and taught a Sunday school class.

When he was 16, Heyer was tremendously moved by a sermon in which Zion's pastor spoke eloquently of the need for home missionaries among the westward-moving American settlers.

Reader 3: When is the last time you heard a pastor preach a sermon calling for young men and women to consider God's call to become a pastor? Why does it happen so infrequently? Are there not just as many opportunities today to proclaim the good news? And are there not has many young people open to the prodding of God's spirit?

Reader 1: Heyer responded enthusiastically. Now in those early days of the 1800s in America, before there were any seminaries, a young man became a pastor the same way he became a furrier: he would apprentice himself to an experienced pastor. In addition, Heyer spent a year as a theological student at a university back in Germany. During the voyage across the ocean, Heyer read a book which predicted the end of the world in 1816; it was a complicated theory which connected Napoleon to a reference in the book of Revelation to "the angel of the bottomless pit" whose Greek name was "Apollyon."

Reader 3: Is there nothing new under the sun? In the 1970s it was Hal Lindsey and *The Late Great Planet Earth*. In 1991, it was the Persian Gulf war and all the talk about an imminent Armageddon. When will Jesus' words finally sink in for us human beings, that "no one knows the hour?" . . . but that we live every day as if it were the coming of the kingdom.

Reader 1: When Heyer returned to America, he began his work as a home missionary on the western frontier. Now realize that in 1818 the frontier was western Pennsylvania and Maryland!

One night Heyer stayed with a very pious American family who asked him to lead devotions . . . in English! He had no difficulty reading from the English Bible, but when it came time for the free prayer, he froze. He had never before prayed in English!

Reader 2: "I finally saved the day by repeating the Lord's Prayer. But I resolved then and there never again to pray publicly in English."

Reader 1: But English was the language of the frontier, and Heyer, tutored by his wife, eventually became very fluent in it. However, the issue of language would crop up again and again. For many German-Americans, German was the language of piety and religion. In 1815, the Lutheran Church in Pennsylvania refused to receive an Episcopalian rector into its ministry — not because of his theology, but because he couldn't speak German!

Heyer was very adept at reading the signs of the times, not only in his early conversion to English, but also in the way he made use of contemporary trends in religion. For example, revivals were a common occurrence on the western frontier and Heyer made use of them as well.

Reader 2: "On the second Thursday in June, 1819, it pleased the Lord to pour out his spirit upon some of the catechumens. It was a day long to be remembered with gratitude and praise . . . The Lord was verily in the midst of us . . . It is remarkable that the arrows of the Almighty were aimed at some of the most wicked characters in this place. They now rejoice that the Lord has snatched them."

Reader 1: The Sunday school movement was another one of Heyer's tools. It had begun in England in 1790, and Heyer was a strong advocate of its value for American Lutherans.

Reader 2: "Dear brothers and sisters, you desire with your whole hearts that your children should be saved. Do not be satisfied merely with praying for their salvation. Do something about it. Join us and give of your time and strength to this good work [of the Sunday schools]."

Reader 3: How does the modern-day pastor/developer go about starting a congregation? As it was for Heyer, today it was done by meeting lots of people. Heyer had to do it on horseback; today the mission developer goes through lots of shoe leather, going door-to-door in new housing developments, extending the invitation to come and worship. Today's mission developer also utilizes the tools of the time; today such tools include direct mail, telephone surveys and advertising.

Reader 1: Mission work among Lutherans in America had been exclusively home missions, that is, the planting of congregations on America's western frontier. But increasingly, the American Lutheran church began thinking about the possibility of sending missionaries to foreign lands. After all, they reasoned, isn't that the way the Lutheran church had begun in America? Way back in 1741 the German pastor, Henry Melchior Muhlenberg, had been preparing himself for mission work in India, but instead he had been sent to America. In 1841, the Lutheran church in America would be celebrating the 100th anniversary of his arrival here. What better way to celebrate than by sending its first Lutheran missionary to India? Heyer, at the age of 48 and recently a widower, eagerly accepted the call. In his farewell letter, he wrote:

Reader 2: "I feel calm and cheerful, having taken this step after serious and prayerful consideration. The smiles of friends have cheered, and the approbation of the churches has encouraged me thus far. But I am aware that, ere long, amidst a tribe of men whose language will be strange to me, I shall behold those smiles only in remembrance, and hear the voice of encouragement only in dying whispers across the ocean; and then, nothing but the grace of God, nothing but a thorough conviction of being in the path of duty, nothing but the approving smile of heaven can keep me from despondency.''

Reader 1: After a six-month voyage across the ocean, Heyer arrived in India. But where and how to begin? European Protestant mission work in India had begun in 1706, and over the years the various churches had staked out their mission fields. But where should Heyer begin this mission work of the American Lutheran church?

He eventually settled upon Guntur, among the Teluga Indians. His decision was strongly influenced by Huddleston Stokes, an Englishman.

Reader 2: ''Here at Guntur we met with a very kind reception from Huddleston Stokes, Esquire, an ardent friend of mission and missionaries, as well as a very exemplary Christian gentleman.''

Reader 1: For Heyer, his acceptance by Stokes was persuasive evidence of a divine call. As it turned out, Mr. Stokes was also a very generous financial supporter of the mission. In fact, without Mr. Stokes' aid, the mission would very likely have failed.

Mission work in India was slow and laborious. At the end of his first year, Heyer had baptized only three adults. The primary thrust of the mission was the establishment of schools, with the hope that the seeds of the gospel could be planted in the children's minds.

We should not forget that preaching the gospel in India was an act of radical social revolution. One could not proclaim the good news of Jesus Christ without also speaking against the social caste system of India, a system which was especially oppressive for the have-nots, the out-castes. It was among these out-castes that Heyer began his work.

Reader 3: Today the gospel still has overtones of radical social revolution. Just listen to our Latin American missionaries as they speak to us about liberation theology, about God's "preferential option for the poor." We here in America may have forgotten just how radical Jesus' message was — both religiously and socially!

Reader 1: Heyer's lifestyle in India was a frugal and ascetic one. He lived as the natives lived. A bowl of rice, curry and tea easily satisfied him. A mat and a blanket on the ground was more than sufficient for a good night's sleep.

There were many back home in America who felt that the progress was slow ... and too expensive. They had spent $5,500 on the India mission field in four years! Could not that money have been better spent on home missions on the American western frontier?

Reader 3: How do you resolve that issue — home missions or foreign missions? Do you feed the hungry by contributing to your local food shelf or by giving to famine relief efforts in the Horn of Africa? In our congregations today we can find advocates on both sides of that issue.

Mission is not a matter of "either/or," but rather "both/and." The book of Acts tells us that, yes, charity and mission begin at home, "in Jerusalem," which was "home" for Jesus' disciples. But it doesn't end there. Rather it spreads to "all Judea and Samaria and to the end of the earth."

Reader 1: During Heyer's second tour of duty in India, he concentrated his efforts in Gurzala, mainly because of the efforts of a native Indian Christian by the name of Weaver John. When Heyer arrived in this village, he found 125 people waiting to be baptized by him. Weaver John held up a small book in his hands, a Teluga translation of the gospel, and he said to Heyer:

Reader 2: "From this book, sir, we date the beginning of the gospel light to our midst. You gave it to me about four years ago, before you went back to your country. Since that time it has pleased the Lord to enlighten us more and more. Some of our children have learned to read and a number of people desire that you should administer the rite of Christian baptism to them."

Reader 1: After spending 16 years in India, Heyer returned to America, and at the age of 64 again took up the challenge of home missions, this time in the state of Minnesota. He traveled to Red Wing, St. Paul, Owatonna, Rochester and many other places, establishing congregations along the way.

Even in those days it took a lot of money to start a new congregation, especially when it came time to erect a church building. When Heyer was pastor of Trinity Lutheran Church in St. Paul, he spoke about his own stewardship and contribution to the building fund.

Reader 2: "Dear friends, the first $500 which I paid, you may regard as my tobacco money. It is meant this way: 50 years ago, like many other boys, I could have begun smoking cigars, which would annually have cost me about $10; thus, in 50 years, without counting interest, $500. But I never had a cigar in my mouth, nor have I spent money for tobacco in any other form; thus I have saved money.

"Those other $500 paid toward the church fund you may regard as my liquor money. I have never made use of the insidious drink; so, in 50 years I have saved much. I have children and grandchildren some of whom are poor, and who would have been delighted had I divided this money among them. But then, they smoke and use alcohol; therefore I do not consider it proper for me to give them this money which I have saved, just to see them smoke and drink it away.

"I thus hand it over to this congregation, on the following condition: until Christmas, 1870, no interest should be paid on the $1,000. But from Christmas, 1870, onward, this

107

congregation shall annually at Christmastime distribute $60 worth of flour, wood and clothing among the poor widows and orphans of the parish.''

Reader 1: We have already heard how, at the age of 77, Heyer made his third and final tour of duty as a missionary to India. He then returned to America, almost 80 years old, and became a housefather at the Lutheran Seminary in Philadelphia, living in the dormitory and becoming the loveable, grandfatherly man on campus. It was here that he died, on November 7, 1873.

During the last years of his life he had become known as Father Heyer. It was a term of endearment, signifying respect and appreciation. Yet from our perspective today, he is also very much the father of American Lutheran missions.

Bibliography

E. Theodore Bachmann, *They Called Him Father: The Life Story of John Christian Frederick Heyer,* Philadelphia: Muhlenberg Press, 1942.

George Drach, *Father Heyer, Pioneer Foreign Missionary,* Baltimore: Board of Foreign Missions, ULCA, 1941.